CONCILIUM

Religion in the Eighties

CONCILIUM

General Secretariat: Prins Bernhardstraat 2, 6521 AB Nijmegen, The Netherlands
Concilium 183 (1/1986): Ecumenism

CONCILIUM

List of Members

Advisory Committee: Ecumenism

Directors:

Hans Küng	Tübingen	West Germany
Jürgen Moltmann	Tübingen	West Germany

Members:

Anna Marie Aagaard	Aarhus	Denmark
Arthur Allchin	Canterbury	Great Britain
Johannes Brosseder	Königswinter	West Germany
Sara Butler MSBT	Philadelphia, PA	U.S.A.
Robert Clément SJ	Hazmieh	Lebanon
John Cobb	Claremont, CA	U.S.A.
Avery Dulles SJ	Washington, D.C.	U.S.A.
André Dumas	Paris	France
Herman Fiolet	Hilversum	The Netherlands
Bruno Forte	Naples	Italy
Alexandre Ganoczy	Würzburg	West Germany
Manuel Gesteira Garza	Madrid	Spain
Adolfo González-Montes	Salamanca	Spain
Catharina Halkes	Nijmegen	The Netherlands
Alisdair Heron	Erlangen	West Germany
Michael Hurley SJ	Belfast	Ireland
Walter Kasper	Tübingen	West Germany
Karl-Josef Kuschel	Tübingen	West Germany
Emmanuel Lanne OSB	Chevetogne	Belgium
Pinchas Lapide	Frankfurt, Main	West Germany
Hervé Legrand OP	Paris	France
Peter Lengsfeld	Münster-Hiltrup	West Germany
Joseph Lescrauwaet MSC	Louvain	Belgium
George Lindbeck	New Haven, Conn.	U.S.A.
Jan Milic Lochman	Basel	Switzerland
Antonio Matabosch	Barcelona	Spain
Harry McSorley	Toronto, Ont.	Canada
John Meyendorff	Tuckahoe, N.Y.	U.S.A.
José Miguez Bonino	Buenos Aires	Argentine
Ronald Modras	St. Louis, Mo.	U.S.A.
Nikos Nissiotis	Ilissia-Athènes	Greece

Daniel O'Hanlon SJ	Berkeley, Cal.	U.S.A.
Wolfhart Pannenberg	Gräfelfing	West Germany
Otto Pesch	Hamburg	West Germany
Alfonso Skowronek	Warsaw	Poland
Heinrich Stirnimann	Fribourg	Switzerland
Leonard Swidler	Philadelphia, PA	U.S.A.
Stephen Sykes	Durham	Great Britain
Lukas Vischer	Berne	Switzerland
Willem de Vries SJ.	Rome	Italy
Maurice Wiles	Oxford	Great Britain
Christos Yannaras	Athens	Greece

CHRISTIANITY
AMONG
WORLD RELIGIONS

Edited by
Hans Küng

and
Jürgen Moltmann

English Language Editor
Marcus Lefébure

T. & T. CLARK LTD
Edinburgh

February 1986
T. & T. Clark Ltd, 59 George Street, Edinburgh EH2 2LQ
ISBN: 0 567 30063 3

ISSN: 0010-5236

Typeset by Print Origination Formby Liverpool
Printed by Page Brothers (Norwich) Ltd

Concilium: Published February, April, June, August, October, December.
Subscriptions 1986: UK: £19.95 (including postage and packing); USA: US$40.00
(including air mail postage and packing); Canada: Canadian $50.00 (including air mail
postage and packing); other countries: £19.95 (including postage and packing).

CONTENTS

Part I
Islam and Christianity

Part II
Hinduism and Christianity

Part III
Buddhism and Christianity

Part IV
Chinese Religion and Christianity

Part V
Towards a Theology of Religions

Synthesis

EDITORIAL

NOBODY CAN deny that we live at a time when the peace of the world and the ability of human beings to live with each other in freedom and justice are constantly undermined by religious tensions. These tensions arise in various ways out of mistrust, and mistrust out of ignorance or arrogance. The adherents of the different religions of the world would be achieving a great deal already if they merely knew more about each other. This is why inter-religious dialogue must in the first place be concerned to widen the horizons of sheer information and understanding.

This ecumenical issue of *Concilium* has set itself ambitious targets in so far as it proposes to set Christianity off against the four great world religions simultaneously. It aims to:

1. look at Christianity in mirrors held up to it by representatives of the four great world religions: Islam, Hinduism, Buddhism and Chinese religion;

2. to take the measure of the challenge posed to Christians by these four great world religions and to do so from the point of view of Christian theologians;

3. to indicate the concrete ways in which Christians and non-Christians are already collaborating with each other in the world.

It goes without saying that we set our contributors a tremendous challenge in asking them to perform their tasks in a few pages. But it seemed important to us as editors to document the full complexity comprehensively and to bring the mutual challenge of Christianity and the world religions to a sharp issue. This, in our opinion, the writers have managed to do to an impressive degree.

We are particularly grateful to our learned *dialogue partners from the other religions*: the Muslim Hossein Nasr (Teheran/Washington), the Hindu Bithika Mukerji (Benares), the Buddhist Sulak Sivaraksa (Bangkok) and the Chinese Shu-hsien Liu (Taiwan). The *Christian point of view* on these religions is ensured by Anthony Johns (Canberra, Australia), Paulos Mar Gregorios (Delhi), Aloysius Pieris (Sri Lanka) and Julia Ching (Toronto). And the *practical collaboration* is reported by Khalid Duran (Hamburg), Michael von Brück (Madras/Hamburg), Seri Phongphit (Bangkok) and Wang Hsien-Chih (Taiwan).

This number is introduced by another attempt to get to grips with the still controverted notion of 'religion' and by way of conclusion is carried forward on both the Catholic (Paul Knitter, Cincinatti) and the evangelical side (Leroy Rounen, Boston) by means of theological reflections on the notion of a 'theology of religions' as it is now and as it could develop. And the whole enterprise is rounded off by an essay in finding a theologically responsible way of dealing with the truth claim of other religions.

Our hope is that this issue will help Christians and non-Christians towards a mutual knowledge of each other, respect for each other and peace with each other.

Translated by Iain McGonagle

Hans Küng
Jürgen Moltmann

Hans Küng

Introduction:
The Debate on the Word 'Religion'

BEFORE WE engage in a dialogue between religions it is not unimportant that we should clarify the concept of religions we are using. The fact that the term 'religion' is constantly used in everyday speech does not prevent students of comparative religion and theologians from having difficulties about resorting to the concept of religion. Now so far as this number is concerned we are going to remain closer to the colloquial usage, yet we can be justified in doing so to the extent that we have first taken into account the objections against the scholarly use of 'religion' on scientific (W.C. Smith) or theological (Karl Barth) grounds and then given religion a more precise definition.

1. Arguments against the Term 'Religion' Insufficient

a. 'Religion' was still used in the middle ages and in the time of the Reformation to designate true 'piety' ('religosity') and not a system of belief that made it possible to discern a true from a false system. From the sixteenth century onwards, however, the word came to be used in the plural, and it referred increasingly to Islam as well as to the ever better known traditions of India and the Far East (especially Hinduism, Buddhism, Confucianism, Taoism and Shintoism).

The question that naturally arose was whether the application of the concept of religion to such varied movements and attitudes of belief did not lead to precipitate generalisations and all too technical (and often abstract) considerations that abstracted from the concrete faith of people in multifarious cultural contexts. This, at any rate, is what one of the best-known students of comparative religion in our time, the Canadian *Wilfrid Cantwell Smith*, maintains.

Smith is perfectly right to keep on impressing on us that a falsely objectifying understanding of religion that considers Islam, Hinduism, Buddhism, Confucianism and the other 'religions' as fixed entities and abstract systems of propositions falls short of reality. For religion is always a matter of concrete, living human beings who—even if they are hardly aware of the fact—are smitten by it at the very heart of their existence (and not merely in their intellect). Human beings do not have religion, they are religious beings, and in very different ways at that. Anybody who gets into conversation with somebody of another faith, let alone lives with him or her, grasps that the other's whole view of reality, life, world and therefore his or her motivation, attitudes and even behaviour are quite different. There is no being first human to which is then added—by way of a plus or an accident, ornament or luxury—being Christian, Muslim, Hindu or Buddhist. No, there is only a being human in a Christian, Islamic Hindu or Buddhist way. And this is not because human beings are from the outset religious, but because religion is from the outset human.

Is there, then, no word to replace a term that can be so easily misunderstood as religion? So far no such word has gained general acceptance. And it is practically impossible to give up an overall concept—even Smith occasionally uses it. So even today the terms 'religion' or 'religions' continue to be used as before, in continuity with everyday practice—it serves better than intellectualistically narrowed expressions such as 'doctrine' or 'opinion' used in the antique and the medieval Church; it is better than the equally narrowed expressions 'faith' or 'forms of faith' central only in prophetic religions (for which there is no plural in German and some other languages); and finally it is better than the newer, rather vague expressions like 'ways' or 'paths' (which soft-peddle the dogmatic aspect). So in the end everything depends on the sense in which the word 'religion' is used. What matters is the reality, not the word. Religion in a comprehensive sense signifies the 'objective' as well as the 'subjective' dimension, what Smith calls the 'cumulative traditions' (as it were the observable 'exterior' of religion in the form of doctrine, ritual, structures, art) as well as what he calls the living, 'personal faith' (the not directly observable but experienced and accessible 'interior' of religion).

b. Contrariwise, certain representatives of Christian theology have advanced objections against the understanding of Christian faith as religion on genuinely theological grounds. They have done so in the wake of the great Protestant theologian *Karl Barth* and the 'dialectical theology' after the First World War. From a different viewpoint than Smith's the application of the term to Christianity for them derogated from its originality. For there was a fundamental and irreconcilable opposition between the revelation of God that was meant to be appropriated in faith (as undeserved gift of God) and religion (as a pious work of human beings). This was still Barth's position in volume I/2 (1948) of his monumental *Church Dogmatics*: religion is to be rejected as human contrivance, idolatry, yes as *unfaith* to the extent that it seeks to justify and hallow itself in face of a God conceived of as capricious and despotic: religion is *the* pursuit of the godless human being! Religion is true and nothing but the Christian faith, of which the Church is the locus, to the extent that it is a response to God's revelation (God's judging and reconciling presence in the world). In effect, neither religion in its objective sense, nor religious rites and practices, institutions and dogmas constitute being a Christian. Faith alone, Christian faith and life that arises out of faith makes the Christian a Christian.

Is there such faith only in Christianity? Is only faith lived in a Christian way genuine faith? And what of the faith of Muslims and Buddhists? At any rate the distinction between the revelation of God appropriated in faith and religion as a pious work of human beings could not be sustained either on scientific or theological grounds. From a theological point of view we cannot from the outset exclude the possibility of what even Karl Barth finally had to admit in the last part of his unfinished *Dogmatics* that he did complete, volume IV/3 (1959), namely, that other religions are also 'light' and—at least indirectly—have something to do with God's revelation, grace and belief, just as, the other way round, Christianity in its varied human manifestations undoubtedly has certain features in common with other religions. From the standpoint of comparative religion at any rate the Christian faith cannot from the outset be set up as an absolute: Christianity is only one religion among many.

This is the sense in which the colloquial use of the word religion is justifiable so far as Christianity as well as the non-Christian religions are concerned.

2. What is Religion?

The definition of religion is as elusive as that of art. The *concept of religion* is not quite an equivocal one, it is rather an analogous one that includes dissimilar things within it. The dissimilarity comes out in the fact that the concept has to take in anything from belief in many gods, through belief in one God to rejection of a belief in God at all (early Buddhism). At the same time, there are also similarities.

Religion always has something to do with the experience of an *'encounter with the holy'* (R. Otto, F. Heiler, M. Eliade, G. Mensching)—whether this 'sacred reality' is thought of as a power, as powers (spirits, demons, angels), as a personal God, (impersonal) divinity or somehow definitive reality (Nirvāna, Shūnyatā, Tao). As a result 'religion' can be described as follows: religion is a *living socio-individuated realisation* (in doctrine, conduct and above all ritual) *of a relationship with something that goes beyond or enfolds human beings and their world and that prolongs itself into a tradition and in a community*—something that is always understood to be the ultimately true reality (God, the Absolute, Nirvāna, Shūnyatā, Tao). Tradition and community are fundamental dimensions for all the great religions. Transcendence (whether inward or outward, in space and/or time, is redemption, enlightenment or liberation) is part of its basic structure.

Religion is anything but a purely theoretical affair, or a matter of the past, a task for discoverers of origins or specialists in sources. No, religion as we understand it here, is *life lived*, inscribed in the hearts of human beings and therefore something of intensely present and daily relevant importance for all religious people. It is, of course, possible to live religion in this sense in a rather traditional, superficial and passive, or in a deeply felt, committed, dynamic way: religion is a conscious-unconscious *believing view of life, attitude towards life, way of living life.* One could call it a socio-individuated ground pattern of human life and the world in virtue of which we (only part consciously) see and experience, think and feel, deal with and suffer everything we do: a transcendentally grounded and immanent, outworking system of coordinates by which we orientate ourselves intellectually, emotionally and existentially. Religion concretely mediates a pervasive sense of life, guarantees ultimate values and unconditioned standards, creates a spiritual community and homeland.

Where such a system of coordinates, such a ground pattern, such a view and form of life is not transcendentally founded, however, is not related to something that goes beyond and enfolds human beings, an absolute or ultimately true reality, but refers to something purely finite, purely human, this-worldly, relative and yet is set up absolutely ('science', 'the party', the 'Führer', 'the material') it is better, in order to avoid misunderstanding, to speak not of religion but (with Paul Tillich) of *quasi-religion*: communism and National Socialism or progress have served as such quasi-religions. And in order to bring out the surrogate character one can also speak of *pseudo-religions*, where one does not from the outset want to impute unworthy intentions to everybody. Where one wants to stress the subjective inwardness of quasi-religion, one can appropriately speak of superstition rather than of faith, whether what is referred to *is* belief in a party, a Führer, science or progress. One may also refer to the objective manifestations as *para-religious*, whether it is a question of party congresses, or the cult of the Führer, or of particular norms or traditions.

The aim of this ecumenical issue is to promote *dialogue* between religions and above all dialogue between Christianity and the world religions. The concept of world religions is itself not unequivocally demarcated and is here used more pragmatically to refer to those religions that have a particular importance on account of their liveliness, diffusion and membership. On this basis, the 'great' world religions . include, besides Christianity, *Islam, Hinduism, Buddhism* and *Chinese religion.* For reasons of space the contributors to this issue have to concentrate on the dialogue between Christianity and these four religions. Likewise Judaism—which must count as a spiritual world power even though it comprises only 0.4% of the world population—cannot come into our present purview, since the Christian-Jewish dialogue presents certain specific problems to do with the origin of Christianity in Judaism, as we have already shown in detail in two previous issues of *Concilium*, one devoted generally to 'Christians and Jews' in 1974 and one to the 'Holocaust as Event of Interruption' in 1984.

Translated by John Maxwell

PART I

Islam and Christianity

Seyyed Hossein Nasr

The Islamic View of Christianity

1. THE TRADITIONAL VIEW OF CHRISTIANITY

IN CONSIDERING the vast subject of the Islamic view of Christianity it is important to bear in mind the presence of an Islamic doctrine concerning Christianity rooted in the Quran and *Hadith*, the Muslims' continuous experience of living with Eastern Christians for fourteen hundred years, over a millenium of battle with a West which for most of that period was Christian and the diversity of the experience of various parts of the Islamic world during the European domination of the colonial period which in any case cannot be divorced in the Muslim mind from Christianity. It is also essential to bear in mind the hierarchic structure of the Islamic revelation in the sense that it possesses levels of meaning ranging from the most exoteric to the most esoteric and the grades of those who attach themselves to the religion to which the Quran itself refers as those who follow the injunction of the religion, *al-islām*, those who possess faith in its more inward sense, *al-imān*, and those who possess spiritual virtue, *al-ihsān*. The attitude of Muslims belonging to these various categories vis-a-vis other religions and especially Christianity has never been the same. Muslim saints and even philosophers have had Christian disciples or teachers while a certain religious authority living in the same city at the same time may have been writing polemics against Christians. Likewise, Muslims living in a particular area without much contact with Christianity have held a different attitude toward Christians than those who fought against the Crusaders, or were expelled from Spain or were put under various kinds of pressures by Christian missionaries.

3

Nevertheless, despite these geographical and historical variations, there remains the Islamic view of Christianity rooted in certain chapters of the Quran mostly dealing with Christ and the Virgin Mary and remaining as a permanent background for Muslim reflections upon the religion which from the beginning was considered to be the closest to Islam not only in time in the historic unfolding of the Abrahamic religions but also in structure and beliefs. In contrast to Christianity which obviously does not possess a specifically Christian doctrine of Islam rooted in its Sacred Scripture, Islam possesses its own revealed knowledge of Christianity, a knowledge which has been interpreted over the ages on many levels from the juridical and theological to the gnostic and mystical but which nevertheless has remained over the centuries as the central determining factor in the way Muslims have viewed Christianity. Even today one cannot gain an in-depth understanding of the Islamic view of Christianity without knowledge of what the Islamic tradition, based upon the Quranic revelation, has taught the Muslims about the religion of Christ.

This traditional Islamic view of Christianity is founded first of all upon accepting *Christianity as a religion revealed by God*, of Christ as being sent by Him and even possessing miraculous characteristics including his virgin birth[1] and of the gospels as being a revealed book. Hence, Christianity became juridically and theologically accepted as a *'religion of the book'* and the Christians as *'the people of the book'* (*ahl al-kitab*) with all that such a status implied for them according to the Divine Law (*al-Shari'ah*)[2] of Islam including the recognition and protection of their religion wherever and whenever they would be under Muslim rule. The Islamic view of Christianity possesses of course its own doctrine of *Christ*, his mission, his being taken to Heaven in body without suffering death upon the cross and his eschatological role in bringing the present cycle of human history to a close. It also includes clear teachings about *Mary*, the most blessed of women, the only woman mentioned by name in the Quran after whom even a chapter of the Sacred Text is named, and the person who accompanies the soul of blessed Muslim women to paradise. The Quranic and Islamic doctrine of Christ and the Virgin, who moreover, appear nearly always together in the Quran, remains a part of the Islamic religion itself independent of Christianity. But the presence of such teachings cannot but affect the Muslims' views towards Christians, and indeed, over the centuries, despite all the enmity and distrust that has characterised much of the history of the two religions when in confrontation with each other, Islam and all traditional Muslims have continued to revere the two figures who also stand at the heart of the Christian religion.

2. REJECTION OF TRINITY AND INCARNATION

There is, however, on the basis of the acceptance of the Divine Origin of the Christian message and reverance of an exceptional character for Christ and the Virgin, a rejection in the Quran itself of both the doctrine of the Trinity and the incarnation. Since Islam is based on the Absolute and not its manifestations and seeks to return Abrahamic monotheism to its original purity as the religion of the One, any emphasis upon a particular manifestation of the One in the direction of the many is seen by Islam as a veil cast upon the plenary reality of *Divine Unity* which Islam seeks to assert so categorically and forcefully. Therefore, the trinitarian doctrine, not only of certain Oriental churches to which the Quranic account seems to be closer than Western interpretations of the doctrine but of any other kind which would not place the trinitarian relationship below the level of Divine Oneness, is rejected by the Islamic perspective. Needless to say Islam would accept an interpretation of the Trinity which would not in any way compromise Divine Unity, one which would consider the persons of the Trinity to be 'Aspects' or 'Names' of God standing below His Essence which, being the Absolute, must be One without condition and above all relations. Likewise, the idea of a Divine Descent in the form of *incarnation* is excluded from the Islamic point of view. The chapter which is entitled 'Unity' or 'Sincerity' in the Quran and which summarises Islamic beliefs concerning the nature of God is as follows:

Say: 'He God is One.

God, the Self-sufficient Besought of all;

He begetteth not, nor is He begotten,

And none is like unto Him.' (translation of M. Lings)

These verses not only define the Islamic perspective but almost seem to oppose directly the doctrines of the Trinity (*tathlīth*) and incarnation (*hulūl*), both being such an anathema to the Muslim mind, as these doctrines were usually understood in the world in which Islam spread.

The question thus appeared to the earliest Muslims as to why a religion revealed by God through such a major prophet as Christ to a people some of whom the Prophet of Islam met and respected, should possess such teachings which should be so directly opposed to what Muslims consider as the obvious truth concerning the nature of the Divine. Few Muslim theologians of the earlier or even later centuries sought to examine the works of Christian theologians themselves on these issues, especially writings emanating from the Latin Church, while certain Sufis such as Ibn 'Arabī' and many of the Persian Sufi poets saw both the doctrine of Trinity and incarnation as symbolic ways of speaking about the Absolute and Its manifestations without in any way destroying the doctrine of Divine Unity.[3] Moreover, a theologian and Sufi like *al-Ghazzālī* tried expressly to absolve Christ himself from having ever taught either the trinitarian or the incarnationist doctrine, he being a prophet who cannot, according to Islam, but claim God's Oneness without any reserve or compromise.[4]

3.   BELIEF IN ABROGATION

By and large, however, Muslims tended toward the elaboration of the Quranic teaching itself concerning the changes and modifications brought about in the text of earlier revelations as a result of the passage of time and lack of care of the followers of these religions to preserve the actual texts revealed to them, not to speak of purposeful distortions. To this view was added the belief in *abrogation* (*naskh*) according to which a later revelation abrogates an earlier one. Some argued on the basis of this idea that the gospels abrogated the Torah and the Quran the gospels and that with the coming of Christianity all Jews should have embraced Christianity and likewise with the coming of Islam all Christians should have become Muslims. But many perceptive religious thinkers of Islam realised that the doctrine of abrogation could not be applied so simply because in the case of the Quran itself certain verses directly concerned with the Divine Law abrogated earlier verses without the earlier verses becoming false or ceasing to be the Word of God. Moreover, Christians continued to live and practice their religion as did the Jews and both obviously according to God's Will. Therefore, their religion could not simply be dismissed as being abrogated. The commonly held view thus remained one of accepting the Divine Origin of Christianity and that Christians would be saved if they practiced their religion,[5] while there was the general feeling that somehow changes had taken place in the Sacred Scripture of the Christians leading them to such doctrines as that of the Trinity and incarnation, neither of which could have been taught by a prophet of God, as Muslims envisaged the prophetic function in its totality from Adam to the Prophet of Islam.

4.   PROBLEMS WITH CHRISTIAN ETHICS

The Islamic view of Christianity is also as much concerned with the *moral and practical aspects of religion* as with the theological. Here, two very different forms of morality have examined and judged the other in the light of their own precepts and norms. Islam criticises Christianity for not having a Divine Law, a *Shari'ah*, in the strict sense of the term and does not understand why Christianity did not follow Mosaic Law or bring a law of its own. Christianity is seen by Muslims as a religion devoid of an exoterism which then substitutes a message of an essentially esoteric nature as the exoteric thereby creating *disequilibrium in human society*. Christian ethics is seen by Muslims as being too sublime for ordinary human beings to follow, the injction to turn the other cheek being meant only for saints. That is why Sufis call Christ the prophet of inwardness and the spiritual life. But since all human beings are not saints, this Christian morality is seen by Muslims as neglecting the reality of human nature and of substituting an unattainable ideal, as far as the collectivity is concerned, for a realism based on human nature and capable of creating equilibrium for man in his earthly life and felicity in the hereafter based upon this equilibrium.

Nowhere is this opposition of moral views more evident than in the question of *sexuality* which is seen as being tainted with sin in the mainstream of Christian theology especially as it developed in the West while being seen as a sacrament in Islam as long as it is practiced according to the Divine Law. Islam sees the indissoluble, monogamous marriage of Latin Christianity as being certainly a possibility but of not exhausting all the possibilities of human nature. Moreover, Islam opposes celibacy and therefore cannot accept the Christian doctrine of the virtue of celibacy over married life. Muslims are especially surprised when Christians attack the Islamic attitude toward sexuality and such practices as polygamy while in the West, in which Christianity has been the religion of the vast majority, sexual promiscuity is of a dimension inconceivable to a traditional Muslim.

This *lack of realism* in promulgating Christian ethics, is seen by Muslims to be also at the root of the Christian opposition to the world and worldly power. The Muslims have always asked if Christianity is opposed to war and Christ said, 'He who uses the sword shall perish by the sword', then why is it that Christian people over the centuries have not carried out less wars than others and certainly have not shown any more restraint in war than have non-Christians. The whole attitude of Christianity towards the world, whether it be its political and economic aspects or the enjoyments of the flesh, is seen by Islam to contain an ambiguity where the ideal preached and the practice followed have often little to do with each other. This opposition issues in fact from the very different conception of the 'world' in the religious perspectives of Christianity and Islam. "For the Christian 'what is of this world, *ipso facto* takes one away from God'; for the Abrahamic Semites [Muslims and also Jews] 'what takes on away *de facto* from God is of this world alone."[6]

Lest it be thought that the evaluation of Christian morality by Muslims is simply negative, it must be emphasised that for traditional Muslims the ethical teachings of Christ are to be criticised not for being imperfect but for being too exalted to be realised by most human beings and therefore not widely applicable. All Muslims who still remain faithful to their tradition revere and respect the Sermon on the Mount and have great reverence for those who put such sublime teachings into practice. They criticise Christianity on this score in being too spiritual not that it lacks spiritual character. In fact there is a widespread Islamic belief according to which in the Abrahamic cycle of revelations, Judaism represents the Law and the religion of this world; Christianity the Way and the religion of the heart or of the other world; and Islam the synthesis of both in which a balance is created between the Law and the Way, between the demands of the body and of the spirit. It is no accident that Christ plays such an important role in Islamic esoterism, totally independent of historical influences, for he represents the esoteric dimension in the Abrahamic tradition, while Sufism *is* esoterism in Islam which seeks to return to the Unity and synthesis of the religion of Abraham before its particularisation into the Judaic and Christian religions.

5. APPRECIATION FOR CHRISTIANITY

The appreciation of the spiritual nature of Christian morality is especially evident where Muslims live near pious Christians. In lands such as Syria and Egypt as well as the Holy Land before recent tragedies, there was hardly a devout Muslim who did not revere and deeply respect some pious Christian friend or neighbour. Reverance for Christian piety and beauty of soul of certain Christians in daily contact with Muslim constitutes a most important element of the Islamic view of Christianity, one which is often left out of account in theological or historical discussions and also one which unfortunately tends to become destroyed in those lands where the fruit of centuries of harmonious relationship between Muslims and Christians is being destroyed as a result of internal wars as well as intrusion of alien factors and forces.

The appreciation of Christianity is, however, not confined to human contacts on an every day basis. In spite of polemics written by Muslim theologians and jurists, there exists a notable body of Islamic literature, especially in Arabic and Persian, which is based on profound respect for Christianity. Most of this literature is of a mystical nature where Christ plays a crucial role but in a Muhammadan universe. No one can read the poetry of

Hāfiz or Rūmī without becoming immediately aware of the ever present power of the 'breadth of the Messiah' to enliven the soul of man in the same way that the historical Christ brought the dead back to life. One must not forget that a saint like Rūmī had many Christian disciples and even a Christian wife who did not convert to Islam, and that he visited Christian monastaries where he held friendly discourse with monks. It was only a bit over a century ago when in Isfahan, where many Armenians lived across the Zayanderud River from the Muslim quarters, a poet like Hātif could claim that while trying to debate with a Christian concerning the Trinity, he heard from the church bells themselves that there is but one God worshipped by Muslims and Christians alike. Likewise, an Ibn 'Arabī, who hailed from southern Spain where he had encountered numerous Christians, could write many an illuminating page on the Christic reality and its function in the whole cycle of prophecy.[7]

6.   PROBLEMS OF THE COMMON HISTORY

Historical contingencies and events such as the *Crusades and the expulsion of Muslims from Spain* have had of course a great deal of effect upon the view of certain Muslims about Christians, if not Christianity itself. But by and large before the present period Muslims have remained remarkably indifferent to Western Christianity and have not been at all interested in studying it. Accounts of West European Christianity do not appear in Muslim sources until the seventeenth and eighteenth centuries and then in chronicles of Ottoman and Moroccan ambassadors rather than in the works of theologians. In general in these sources some description is given of the institution of the papacy which Muslims did not understand fully and which they usually opposed. In fact something of the anti-clericalism of the French Revolution entered into the Islamic world and even affected those Muslims who were opposed to modernism, but who saw this European anti-clericalism as affirming their own opposition to the presence of a priesthood in Christianity. Again, they contrasted the situation of Islam in which every man is his own priest with that of Christianity, especially Catholic Christianity with an elaborate ecclesiastic hierarchy, and thought of the latter as being a later invention opposed to the original simple teachings of Christ. As Muslims came to know also more about post-medieval religious art of Europe, especially that of the Baroque period with its extremely ornate and naturalistic patterns and designs, they grew in their opposition to the practices of Christians and criticised their possession of power, both economic and military, combined with an art which appeared to Muslim eyes as an idolatry.[8] Such was not the case in either medieval Spain or Byzantium, but then Muslims were facing a Christian civilisation of traditional character, possessing a spirituality and an other worldliness of which the more perceptive among Muslim observers were fully aware.

Likewise, *missionary activity*, whether Catholic or Protestant, usually combined with political and economic domination played a major role in determining Muslim attitudes toward Christians to the extent that in the Arab world to this day missionary activity (*tabshīr*) is practically identified with colonialism (*istī'mār*). Since the Western powers while opposing religion within their borders usually helped the missionaries from their countries when they went abroad, most Muslims came to identify practically all the activities of western powers with Christianity. A distrust was created of Western Christianity which did not exist during the Crusades when European nations were openly Christian. This distrust has become aggravated as a result of political machinations and such collosal tragedies as recent events in Palestine and Lebanon. As a result, an atmosphere of bitterness has been created in many quarters vis-à-vis Christianity, an atmosphere which did not exist even half a century ago and certainly not in the Middle Ages when Christians and Muslims often fought, but as enemies who respected each other.

To these negative elements must be added the *rise of* what in the West is called *Islamic fundamentalism*. Many of the movements grouped under this name have in fact much in common with modernism and are not to be confused with traditional Islam. One of the major points of difference between them is in fact in their attitude towards Christianity. To the extent that these movements, many of which are fanatical and seek to redress grievances through violence, spread among traditional Muslims, the base of faith of the Muslims who accept their rhetoric and so-called idealogy becomes narrowed. A simple peasant in the countryside of Tunisia or a merchant in the Lahore bazaar is usually more open to Christianity and appreciative of its spiritual values than an educated Muslim student caught in the web of one of such so-called fundamentalist movements. The fire of hatred burns bonds of amity and shrivels the soul of the faithful whether they be Muslim or Christian.

7. COEXISTENCE AND MUTUAL ACCEPTANCE

There are, however, those within the Islamic world who realise that the destinies of Islam and Christianity are intertwined, that God has willed both religions to exist and to be ways of salvation for millions of human beings, that the enemy of both religions is modern agnosticism, atheism and secularism, and that Christianity is a dispensation willed by Heaven not only as a historical background to Islam but as a revelation destined to guide a sector of humanity until the second coming of its founder. Such Muslims can draw from a vast resource of traditional Islamic writings which is able to provide ample basis for a veritable ecumenical encounter with Christianity based not on reducing each religion to a bare minimum to accommodate the other, but grounded in that transcendent unity which unites all authentic religions, and especially Christianity and Islam. Such Muslims, far from surrendering to the fads and fashions of the day in the name of keeping up with the times, or of loosening the reins which control the passions in order to express anger in the name of indignation, base themselves on the eternal message of the Quran in their dealing with Christians. They develop, in the light of present needs, the expressly Quranic doctrine of the universality of revelation and even practice the Christian virtue of turning the other cheek when it comes to the matter of religious truth, that is, they accept the validity of Christianity even if Christians deny the authenticity of the Islamic revelation. They let the matter of who is saved be decided by the Supreme Judge who judges according to the truth not the 'fashions of the times' and expediency. The voice of such Muslims might seem to be drowned out at the moment by the cry and fury of those who preach hatred in the name of justice and who even insult other religions in direct opposition to the injunctions of the Quran. But the voice of understanding and harmony cannot but triumph at the end for it is based upon the truth and surely Christ whose second coming is accepted by both Christians and Muslims shall not come but in truth and shall not judge but by truth, that truth which he asserted himself to be, according to the Gospel statement, and which the Quran guarantees as being triumphant at the end for there will finally arrive the moment when it can be asserted with finality that 'the Truth has come and falsehood has perished'. (XVIII; 81).

Notes

1. References to Jesus and Mary abound in the Quran. See especially *Sūrahs* III, V, XIX, and LXI.
2. There is an extensive literature on the legal status of *dhimmah* and *dhimmīs* especially Christians. As far as the Western views of the subject are concerned, see C. Chéhata *Essai d'une théorie générale de l'obligation en droit musulman* (Cairo 1936); and R.B. Rose 'Islam and the development of personal status laws among Christian *dhimmīs*' *Muslim World*, 72 (1982) 159-179. Muslims are in general very sensitive to

the Christian criticism of the Islamic law of *dhimmīs* and nearly all Muslim apologetic literature from Amīr 'Alī onward contains discussions of this subject.

3. In his *Tarjumān al-ashwāq*, trans. R.A. Nicholson, London, 1978, p.70, Ibn 'Arabī has a poem which is as follows:

My Beloved is three although He is One, even as the (three) Persons (of the Trinity) are made one Person in essence.

In his own commentary upon the poem (*ibid.*, p.71) he adds, 'Number does not beget multiplicity in the Divine substance, as the Christians declare that the Three Persons of the Trinity are One God, and as the Koran declares (XVII, 110): '*Call on God or call on the Merciful; howsoever ye invoke Him, it is well, for to Him belong the most excellent Names.*' The cardinal Names in the Koran are three, viz. Allāh, al-Rahmān and al-Rabb, by which One God is signified, and the rest of the Names serve as epithets of those Three.'

In his *al-Futūhāt al-makkiyyah*, 3, Beirut, (n.d.), p.172, Ibn 'Arabī states that the Christians in emphasizing the Trinity still have a way open to God's uniqueness (*al-fardāniyyah*) since the number three is in a sense a return to the number one, and trinity being the first reflection of unity in the domain of multiplicity.

4. See his *al-Radd al-jamīl alā sarīh al-injīl*, trans. R. Chidiac, Paris, 1939. Some contemporary scholars have doubted the authenticity of the attribution of this work to al-Ghazzālī, while L. Massignon and several other scholars consider it to be one of al-Ghazzālī's authentic writings. In any case the work exemplifies the attitude we wish to point out.

5. There were some Muslim religious authorities who did not accept this view, but the majority of them as well as of traditional Muslims in general have believed and continue to believe that the doors of both heaven and hell are open for Christians as they are for Muslims. Moreover, there are numerous *hadīths* concerning both Christ and Moses leading the virtuous members of their community to paradise on the Day of Judgement. The general use of the term *kāfir* (usually translated as infidel) so common in Muslim sources when referring to Christians is more a custom than a strictly speaking theological definition. Some Muslim schools of thought have called their Muslim opponents *kāfirs* as well without this implying damnation in principle as the doctrine of *Extra ecclesiam nulla salus* would imply.

6. F. Schuoun *Christianity/Islam—Essays on Esoteric Ecumenism*, trans G. Polit (Bloomington, Indiana, 1985) p.111.

7. See especially his *Bezels of Wisdom*, trans. A.W.J. Austin, New York, 1980, chapter XV 'The Wisdom of Prophecy in the Word of Jesus'; and Ibn 'Arabī *La Sagesse des Prophètes*, trans. T. Burckhardt (Paris 1955) pp.109-129.

8. This kind of reaction was not to be observed to the same extent as far as Protestantism was concerned. Many Muslims, who in fact encountered Protestantism for the first time, thought that it was closer to Islam and that Luther had moved in the direction of the Islamic understanding of religion.

Anthony Johns

Islam as a Challenge to Christianity

THE CHALLENGE of Islam is total—it presents itself as the primordial authentic religion par excellence. The final, complete form in which this religion lives and is taught today is guaranteed by the Qur'an, the book revealed to Muhammad by an angel. It proclaims the God of Abraham, Isaac and Jacob, who first revealed himself to Adam, father of mankind, and made a covenant with him and his descendents. This covenant is dramatically presented in the Qur'an in Chapter 7 verse 172. All of Adam's future progeny are drawn from his loins at the beginning of time, and God has them testify in response to his question: 'Am I not your Lord?' They reply 'Yes, indeed, we so testify' thereby formally accepting a responsibility which would entail reward for faithfulness and punishment for default. The covenant was re-presented and renewed over the generations by a series of prophets sent by God, many of whom are identified by names known from the Old Testament, including some not usually regarded as prophets in the Judaeo-Christian tradition, for example, Joseph and Solomon. Others such as Hud and Salih are known only in the Arabian Tradition.

1. I. MUHAMMAD

The man who presented the covenant in its final form, safe-guarded from any corruption or loss, to endure until the end of time is Muhammad, who was born in Mecca about 570 A.D. and died in Medina in 632 A.D., a city about 200 miles to the north of his birthplace. Muslims see him as descended from Abraham through Ismael, and as the eschatological prophet foretold by Moses in Deuteronomy. According to the traditional accounts, Muhammad was a merchant, a man of the world, but at the same time one of integrity, prayer and reflection. He was called to be a *prophet* at the age of forty, by an overwhelming presence which came upon him while meditating in a cave in the hills near Mecca, when the first words of the Qur'an were revealed to him (chapter 96, verses 1-5) as a divine command:

Declare in the name of God who created!

Created man from a clot of blood!

Declare—your Lord is most Gracious

He taught man by the Pen

Taught him what he did not know.

He lived the rest of his life in the shadow of this primal experience, and a series of new revelations was brought to him at intervals, on occasions for which they were appropriate. Guided and inspired by these revelations he preached, denouncing idolatry, the exploitation of the widow and the orphan, and warning of an inexorable day of judgement which would bring the punishment of the wicked, and the reward of the good.

In *Mecca* he achieved only a limited success. In 622, therefore, he migrated to *Medina* with his followers as leader of a community based not on blood relationship, domicile, or race, but on belief in one God, and his role as leader and lawgiver to that community. In this community there was to be no distinction between the sacred and the secular—to pray, to fast, to give alms was as much a matter of positive law, as the prohibition to steal, to commit adultery, to give false witness. During the years at Medina the emphasis of revelations that continued to be brought to him shifted to matters relevant to the needs of the social and ritual life of the community—criminal law, inheritance, divorce, the rites of the pilgrimage, but did not neglect those which concerned him whether as leader of the community or simply as a human being—in his arguments with his enemies, in problems which affected his personal life, even in such mundane matters as his relationships with his wives. In 630 he returned in triumph to Mecca his native city, having won all but universal acceptance of the two brief sentences: 'There is no god but the God, and Muhammad is his messenger' that was the cornerstone of the Muslim community. Thereafter Mecca was the city of God, and Medina the city of the prophet, from which he ruled his nascent State.

2. THE QUR'AN AND THE HADITH

The Qur'an comprises the utterances brought to Muhammad by the angel Gabriel over the period of his life as a Prophet. After his death they were organised into 114 chapters sub-divided into verses and made into a book between two covers. They are not arranged according to chronology or topic, but in order of decreasing length. Although some, particularly the shorter chapters of only a few verses, have a single or dominant theme, for the most part they are a mosaic of legal provisions, of threats and promises, of exhortations, stories, arguments and prayers, often echoing and re-echoing each other.

The resulting slim volume, about the length of the New Testament, is for Muslims *the uncreated word of God*, brought down from 'the mother of the Book' beneath the divine throne. The printing or writing of the Arabic characters representing the divine words on the pages of any copy of the Qur'an infuses them with holiness, and renders every page itself sacred. It should not be touched by anyone not in a state of ritual purity. No piece of paper with even a verse of the Qur'an on it, or simply the name of God, may be treated with disrespect. The most striking expression of love for and joy in these words is revealed in the art of Qur'anic recitation, it is one of the great achievements of the human voice, in which every word and phrase is cradled lovingly on the tongue and lips of the reciter.

Next in sanctity to the word of God in the Qur'an are *the words of Muhammad as a man*—his explanations of the meaning of the Qur'an, elaborating points of law and ritual only handled tangentially in the Qur'an, and recording his views on and actions in virtually every area of human life and activity ranging from prayer, details of personal hygiene, and dietary preferences to the principles of diplomacy. These sayings, known as *hadith* exist in six canonical collections, each containing upwards of 18,000 sayings. Taken together they serve both to give a detailed picture of the conduct of Muhammad as a man—the most perfect of men, whose life should serve as a model to be imitated in every detail, and to supply the second great source of Islamic Law.

3. THE FAITH AND PRACTICE OF ISLAM

From the Qur'an and *hadith* are derived the content of three key terms in the Muslim's understanding of the religion:

The first is *Islam*. It comprises *five* ritual acts regarded as the *pillars of the religion*—the declaration 'There is no god but the God, and Muhammad is His Messenger', the two sentences by which one accepts membership of the Muslim community, becomes subject to the Law, and renews one's faith and commitment to God and his prophet; the performance of the five daily ritual prayers, at dawn, noon, mid-afternoon, sunset and night; keeping the fast of Ramadan—the ninth month of the Muslim lunar year—by abstaining during the hours of daylight from food, drink (including smoking) and sexual activity; payment of the poor tax, and participating in the rites of the pilgrimage at Mecca in the twelfth month of the Muslim year at least once in a life-time, if one has the legitimate means to do so.

The second is *Iman*, an inward commitment to belief in God, His prophets, His angels, His Books, and His power of predestination for good and ill.

The third is *Ihsan*, usually translated as righteousness, and this in the words of a famous saying of Muhammad is that 'You should serve God as though you see him, for even if you do not see him, he sees you'.

It is characteristic of the religion that there is a progression from the outward observance of ritual acts, to an inward faith that leads finally to an immediate and continuing sense of the presence of God.

Of *the pillars of Islam*, two are especially relevant for the purposes of this essay: prayer and fasting. (a) The first one is the *obligation of prayer*. The duty to pray is proclaimed publicly, by the muezzin, and in the domain of Islam, from Morocco to Indonesia, one is never away from the call to prayer:

God is most Great
God is most Great
I testify there is no god but the God
and that Muhammad is the messenger of God
Come to prayer
Come to security
(at dawn)
Prayer is better than sleep
God is most Great.

This *ritual prayer* is at once an act of worship, of self-dedication, or turning away from sin, and of petition—for one's self and the Muslim community, for the living and the dead.

Central to it is the opening chapter of the Qur'an, al-Fatiha:

In the name of God, the Merciful the Compassionate.
Praise is God's due, the Lord of the Worlds
The Merciful, the Compassionate.
Lord of the Day of Judgement.
It is you we worship, you we ask for aid.

Guide us along the right path.
the path of those you bless not that of those against whom
is your anger, not that of those who go astray.

It is to utter such expressions of worship that Muslims rise at dawn, and family members, friends and individuals interrupt the daily routine of work or leisure.

(b) The other is the *fast of Ramadan*. It is observed as an act of obedience to a command of God himself in the Qur'an (chapter 2, verse 183): 'You who believe, a fast is prescribed for you as it was prescribed for those who went before you, so that you may grow in devotion'. The physical demands alone of the fast are vigorous, but outward obedience is not enough. The month should be spent prayerfully, and every sinful thought an inclination be suppressed, otherwise its goals, which are to purify the mind and bring worldly desires under control will not be achieved.

In a special way, this fast both demonstrates the identity of the Muslim community, and confers on it a profound sense of unity, beginning with the closest members of the family. The main social event of the day, the breaking of the fast heightens this sense of community, when friends, acquaintances and family members come together to each others' houses to share in the sense of relief and thanksgiving that a day's fast has been successfully completed— just as at the end of the fasting month the whole community comes together to offer a mass public prayer of thanksgiving, ask pardon of each other for the faults and failings of the past year, with the resolution to make a fresh start for the new one.

4. CHALLENGES TO CHRISTIANITY

(a) Scripture

The Qur'an, for Muslims, has an authenticity and therefore authority that does not belong to the scriptures of Judaism and Christianity in the form in which they exist today. In the Muslim view the books of the *Old Testament*, since they have undergone redaction, have been diluted by human agencies, and in part, at least, their teaching has been distorted. In particular, passages relating to the future coming of Muhammad have been removed, and quite falsely, divinity has been attributed to *Jesus*. The Qur'an sees him as a *prophet like Muhammad, though of a lower rank*, to whom a book was given. He speaks in the cradle, saying 'I am a servant of God; he has given me the Book, and made me a prophet' (chapter 19, Mary verse 30). Since the gospels in their present form are about Jesus, clearly they are not the book the Qur'an says was given to Jesus, and are thus unreliable. In chapter 5, The Table, verse 17, the Qur'an denounces the divinity attributed to him: 'Those who say that Allah is the Messiah, the son of Mary, are infidels. Declare: Who has any power against God, even if he wished to destroy the Messiah, the son of Mary, his mother, and everyone on the earth.'

In chapter 4, Women, verse 171 the Qur'an says: 'The Messiah, Jesus the son of Mary is the messenger of God, His word that he addressed to Mary, and a spirit from him. So believe in God and his messengers, and do not say "A Trinity" . . . God is one God. Far be it from him that he should have a son.' In verse 157 of the same chapter the reality of the crucifixion is denied: 'They (the Jews) say we, indeed we killed the Messiah the son of Mary. They did not kill him and they did not crucify him, but it was made to appear to them (as though they had).'

For Muslims then, *Jesus is solely man* even though directly formed in the womb of Mary by the creative word of God since the Qur'an speaks with an authority that the gospels attributed to the Evangelists lack.

(b) Theology

It is largely on the basis of this Christology that Islam elaborates its theological challenge to Christianity which may be expressed succinctly as follows. *God is one*, all-powerful, all-knowing, all-seeing, the Creator, the Destroyer; he brings to life and he slays and can bring about the resurrection. To man, he is the merciful, the compassionate. In the light of this theology of unity, the Christian doctrine of a three-personed God, Father, Son and Spirit is not only confusing, but scandalous.

This God, although closer to man than his jugular vein, is utterly transcendent. *Creation* is the work of God. It provides signs of his existence. The Qur'an gives as irrefutable arguments for the existence of God the movement of sun, moon and stars in their courses, the cycle of the seasons, the marvel of conception, gestation and birth of all species, and the riches of the earth and sea put at the disposal of man. These signs however, do not reveal his nature. Thus since the nature of God transcends what can be known by reason, right and wrong are to be discovered and understood through the Law revealed in the Qur'an, not by reason. Although not irrational, the Law does not need or depend on the justifications that reason can give.

The Qur'an tells of the *disobedience of Adam and Eve* in the Garden. But this act of disobedience, although it results in their banishment from the Garden, does not result in an inherited flaw. Man is born in a natural state of goodness which, despite his weakness, he can maintain by accepting God's will and guidance. If he is disobedient, the harm done is to himself; if he is obedient, then the reward is of God's bounty, not because man has any claim on him. God created man out of a wisdom beyond human understanding. He sent messengers to teach him. At the end of time God will resurrect and judge him. The ultimate argument for the resurrection in the Qur'an is that what God has done once, he can do again. There is no need for an act of *redemption*, and it is perhaps to remove any residual idea of redemptive suffering that might adhere to the figure of Jesus, that the Qur'an denies the crucifixion.

It may thus be seen how in making its challenge, Islam takes some of the terms, figures, symbols and events that serve to identify Christianity, and highlight its cosmological, meta-historical character, but altered their meaning and function. The result is a *different economy of salvation*, justified by a repetitive rather than cumulative understanding of revelation.

5. CHRISTIAN RESPONSES

(a) To the challenge of Muslim scripture and theology

Christians do not concede the *authority the Qur'an* claims for itself. For them, in whatever the word 'inspired' is understood, the bottom line is that the book is Muhammad's. Nevertheless the theological challenges it presents should be faced honestly out in a positive spirit. What the Qur'an denies is denied because it appeared wayward or even meaningless. At the time of Muhammad there were still bitter controversies among Christians in Byzantium, Syria and Egypt that had their echoes in the great urban centres of western Arabia such as Mecca and San'a concerning an orthodox formula to encapsulate definitively the nature of Christ—was he wholly God, without a human nature, was he wholly man, but one in whom God was present, or was he somewhere in between. The Qur'an's solution is to pull the carpet from under the feet of the quarreling groups by presenting its own doctrines: it denies the divinity of Jesus. He was born of a virgin, but God was not incarnate in him; he was a creature, called to be a prophet, and given a book to preach. As such it is a challenge to that factionalism and arrogance among Christians which hides the message and the person of Jesus, word of God incarnate, behind a smoke-screen of bitter words and intellectual sophistries.

The Qur'an denies the *doctrine of the Trinity*. If this doctrine contains something ineffable about the inner life of the infinite God, this should show in Christian living. It should not be paraded as a formula justified by the words it contains rather than by the inner meaning these words imperfectly express. If the Qur'an has nothing to say about redemption is it because somehow the awe and mystery of the cosmic drama of the infinite God revealed in human form suffering, dying and rising again, has itself been hidden by forms of words that have received official sanction. Such challenges have no authority to subvert the doctrines of Christian belief expressed in the Nicene Creed, but they are a reminder of the way in which familiarity and routine can shut out depths of meaning to which the traditional formulations were designed to give access, and leave them, even to Christians, as empty words, recited out of habit. The Islamic experience of our response to them cannot be ignored.

(b) To the challenge of Muslim ethics

If the challenge of Muslim theology can be creative, even more so can that of Muslim ethics. Popular ideas about Islam attribute to it a rather easy morality, and a disregard for the position of *women*. Western knowledge of Islam hardly goes beyond the provisions it makes for *polygyny*, the ease with which a man may execute divorce, and the dark-eyed houris that await the blessed in heaven. In fact it is precisely in the areas of *individual morality, personal piety, family and community life* that Islam presents challenges to Christians that must be faced, for paradoxical as it may seem, it is in these areas that the world of Islam serves as a mirror in which Christians may look, and there see their strengths, and more often their weaknesses reflected.

The virtues that one sees practised in Muslim communities, and the convictions that underpin them require careful reflection—remembering that ideals are not always reached. There is the *awareness of the presence of God*, who though transcendent sees and judges all, the sense of *gratitude* to him for the gifts of nature, the *faithfulness* to the daily call of the muezzin—to turn aside from work or leisure to pray causes no embarrassment—and the community discipline revealed in the fast. The *sense of community* and close family ties are revealed in a highly developed sense of *hospitality*, personal kindness, and the acceptance of social responsibility. Such values within the extended family and the wider community are of course not exclusive to Islam. Outside the industrialised West, the family unit is still central to life in society. But in many parts of the world it is Islamic values that hold the society together in a time of transition and ensure the loyalty of family members to each other.

This social sense is fortified by the *community of faith*, but it also belongs to the wider context of the *unity of the human family*—all human beings are descended from Adam. Christians share that belief, yet while Muslims have at times been guilty of racial prejudice, nowhere and at no time has any tradition of Islam, mainstream or fringe, given its blessing to the kind of racism that is deeply engrained in so many northern Europeans, let alone to a system as monstrous as that of apartheid in the republic of South Africa.

The moral principles that these qualities reflect derive from the conviction that there is a *single code of morality* that applies to public and private, secular and religious life, and that the ultimate source for the knowledge of right and wrong is God's law. Such matters are not to be decided by majority vote, or fundamental differences tolerated simply as alternative life styles.

CONCLUSION

There is much that Christians may find unacceptable in the formulations and emphases of Islam. The spiritual insights of certain passages in the Qur'an and the sense of near ecstacy that it sometimes expresses are inspiring. Other parts however, particularly those stipulating punishments such as maiming or flogging do not immediately command assent or respect. For many, the thought of an authorised polygyny is abhorrent. *At the same time they will miss certain emphases central to the Christian tradition, such as the sacral and sacramental potential of created things and the work of human hands. This is exemplified in the communion with the Holy enshrined in the ritual sharing of bread and wine which is at the very heart of the central act of Christian worship. So far from having a ritual meaning, wine is forbidden in Islam, and the very act of eating or drinking breaks ritual purity. In such matters there are problems that cannot be resolved in the short term, any more than can the mystery of religious pluralism in the wider sense.*

There is the constant danger that argument on such points of disagreement in attempts to prove by natural reason whose morality is better, will lead to a bitterness, if not downright hatred, destructive of personal relationships. When so much is shared, the primary human responsibility is to seek wisdom in the quality of commitment to the source of every moral sense, God.

Non-Muslims, by definition, do not see the Qur'an and Muhammad in the same light as do Muslims. They cannot refuse to learn from the testimony of Muslim living.

Calid Duran

Christian-Muslim Cooperation
(Examples from Spain to Afghanistan)

IN VIEW of the ceaseless anti-Western hostilities in many parts of the Muslin world one might feel inclined to ask whether there is any perspective at all for Christian-Muslim cooperation. I should like to emphasise, therefore, that there is just as much encouraging news, if not more, than all those well-publicised negative facts.

1. RED CROSS AND CRESCENT

True, in the Spring of 1985 the *Egyptian* government had to pass a law prohibiting the 'war of the stickers'. Copts and Muslims had developed a habit of displaying their religious creed on their cars. Some automobiles seemed to serve more as sectarian campaign trailers than as private vehicles. This is unfortunate indeed, because there was a time, back in 1919, when all Egyptians—Copts and Muslims together—fought for the liberation of their country from foreign domination. In those days they used to demonstrate with flags bearing Crescent and Cross. In retrospect one might deplore that this did not become their national flag.

Today, in *Spain*, white flags bearing a red Crescent and Cross, are a common sight, as if Islam and Christianity had at last merged, after centuries of futile enmity. This apparent syncretism is in reality born out of a very simple necessity. Half a million Muslims, mainly working in France, Belgium and the Netherlands, tend to pass through Spain at this time of the year on their way home to spend their vacations in Northafrica. All along the established 'Route of the Moroccans' the *Spanish Red Cross* and the *Moroccan Red Crescent* join hands and set up mixed First Aid Centres. This resulted in the birth of a new symbol, illustrating unity of purpose of the two religious communities.

Any emphasis on the challenge posed by the African natural calamity must sound platitudinous, and yet it may be time to ponder over the far-reaching effects of this challenge to both religions. Ethiopia, as the country worst affected, has a population that is, roughly speaking, half Christian and half Muslim. Regrettably some of the Western aid appears to be motivated by a distinct commitment to the Christians *qua* Christians, while the oil-rich Arab states sometimes give the impression as if their primary—if not sole—concern were to keep the starving Muslims alive.

As a result of developmental problems Muslims have so far generally lagged behind with regard to such large scale humanitarian efforts. Of late, however, they have made considerable headway in this field. '*Kuwait 1985*' definitely is a landmark in this development. Pride of performance and a new self-assurance are certainly the best guarantees for an emancipation from the confines of narrow confessionalism. Gigantic salvage operations, such as the one presently under way in Africa, might very well turn out to be the cornerstone of a future ecumenical *caritas*. Sooner or later the survival of all of us will depend on this type of Christian-Muslim cooperation.

Until now the most encouraging examples still take the form of local 'miracles' hidden away in the bush. In *Western Kenya*, not far from the border with war-torn Uganda, Muslim elders pulled their resources together and founded the *Mumias Muslim Secondary School*. More than half of the students and teachers are Christians. As such, this school has a model character, for it has come into existence in an area otherwise dominated by missionary schools tending to generate confessional rivalry. The *Mumias Muslim Secondary School* pays for its exemplary ecumenical spirit inasmuch as it does not receive financial assistance from either side, depending entirely on the sacrifices of the founding fathers and the dedicated staff members. If it manages to cross those material hurdles it may well prove a sign-post pointing toward a promising area of Christian-Muslim cooperation. A Nigerian and a Tanzanian bishop, both hailing from families that are partly Christian, partly Muslim, report of similar ecumenical initiatives in their parishes. There is no dearth of such redeeming features, despite an unmistakable rise of fanatical fundamentalism on both sides in many places.

2. AFGHANISTAN AND EUROPE

More than 200 members of the medical professions, almost exclusively from France, have already each spent about a year serving with the *Afghan resistance* in a country ravaged by Soviet occupation forces. The population of this 'medical desert' is entirely Muslim and has always shown a repellent attitude toward everything foreign. However, the Afghans are deeply impressed by the sacrificial spirit of those young Europeans who are risking their life during every moment of their sojorn in the 'liberated areas', sharing the sufferings of a people subjected to the most savage aggression of our times. A delegation of the Afghan resistance recently touring Latinamerica did not miss the opportunity to thank bishops in Bogotá and Buenos Aires for the heroic support rendered to a Muslim people by such a large number of young Christians. Hâshim Zamâni, 'poet of the Afghan resistance', spoke of a new page that has been opened in Christian-Muslim relations.

Hamburg is the headquarters of a *Solidarity Committee for the Afghan People.* Most of its founding members had constituted the team of *Christian-Muslim Dialogue* at the Protestant 'Church-Days' in Nuremberg in 1979. An international congress of Afghanistan support committees was then convened in an institution bearing the intriguing name *Mission Academy* (affiliated to the University of Hamburg). Moreover, this academy put its premises at the disposal of Muslims during Pentecost. Christian theologians at the *Mission Academy* worked untiringly for many years on behalf of the *moros*, a suppressed Muslim minority in the Southern Philippines. The world press occasionally mentions the *moros* as being patronised by Libya, Iran or Saudi Arabia. However, weapons is all that has been coming forth,—surely not the most effective help. Experts at the *Mission Academy* in Hamburg strove hard to preserve *moro* literature and traditions and to make them accessible through the media, thus helping this Muslim minority to maintain its identity. It is partly due to those contributions that the *moros* have developed a new consciousness. They have become aware that their freedom struggle is not a war between Christianity and Islam, but a popular uprising against a corrupt regime that is just as anti-Christian as it is anti-Muslim. In this way the word *Mission* has acquired a new sense, denoting a Christian mission on behalf of Muslims, and viceversa.

The *Interfaith Association*, centred in *England,* is particularly attentive to the violation of human rights in countries such as the Sudan—the survival of which depends on the *modus vivendi* of the Christian and the Muslim segments of the population. Muslim members of *Interfaith* take up the cudgels on behalf of the Southern Sudanese Christians whereas Christian members uphold the cause of persecuted Muslim dissidents. One of the most outstanding religious thinkers of our days, Mahmûd M. Taha, was publicly hanged in Khartoum on January 18, 1985,—as an 'apostate and enemy of God'. Ever since, he is being hailed all over the Muslim world as the greatest mystic saint and 'martyr of the 20th century'. During his lifetime it was *Interfaith Association* that worked hardest to save him.

When Pope John Paul II visited *France, Le Monde* requested the Moroccan writer Tahar Benjelloun, as a prominent spokesman for the Muslim diaspora, to comment upon the visit. Benjelloun was indeed delighted to welcome the Holy Father. He pointed out the fact that in Westen Europe the Church had become a sign of hope for Muslims. Churches even turned into sanctuaries in the literal sense, inasmuch as a number of times Muslims had to take refuge in a church to prevent being expelled from the country. The case of several hundred Moroccans in a Dutch church was only the most striking example. In addition there are the many scholarships granted to Muslim students by various Church bodies, the many hostels run by the churches and numberless other charitable deeds and activities. Benjelloun emphasised a fact that seems to be common to most Western European states: while political parties and trade unions failed the New Muslim work force, the Church proved its mettle, buried old rivalries and came to the rescue of the 'stranger in the land'.

Coming back to *Spain we* find more examples of a pioneer attitude. We are here presented with a kind of laboratory telling us much about the potentials and the eventual direction and shape such Christian-Muslim cooperation is likely to take. This Spanish vanguard is personified by Father Emilio Galindo Aguilar who publishes a magazine on Christian-Muslim *Encuentro*. He is also running a centre called DAREK-NYUMBA (meaning 'Your House' in Arabic and Swahili), catering for all the needs of Christians and Muslims in their interaction—from language courses (Arabic for Spaniards and Spanish for Arabs) to counselling and religious instruction for children of mixed couples. Such activity furnishes dialogue with a solid practical base. Ultimately Father Galindo has started to enunciate what he calls CRISLAM. The theoretical underpinning for this ecumenical movement is derived from Ibn 'Arabī, whom many regard as the greatest mystic of all times (*al-shaikh al-akbar*). Significantly, Ibn 'Arabī hailed from Murcia in Spain.

CRISLAM, however, may not only break through barriers, it may as well draw a dividing line. Quite a few Christians and Muslims, who are otherwise fond of dialogue, will be scared away by what might look to them as an inadmissible syncretism. This may precisely be the difference between dialogue and cooperation for those craving definitions. Nonetheless, the purport of CRISLAM is probably fairly akin to that of the 'universal theology' Christian thinkers such as Leonard Swidler, Hans Küng, Wilfred Cantwell Smith, Raimundo Panikkar and others are heading to. They are keen on sailing forth together with Muslims, especially since they, too, proceed from a humanitarian commitment and the defence of human rights. The activism so much stressed on these pages might be of vital importance especially for the more intellectual forms of dialogue. Manifestly, such activism is not going to smoothen out theological differences, nor are those to be glossed over or hidden under the carpet. However, the activism of Christian-Muslim cooperation is bound to instil interreligious talks with new vitality and prevent them from falling victim to professionalisation and inbreeding.

3. FUTURE PERSPECTIVES

Luckily, there are those 'heavenly' circles of academics getting together every now and then in places such as the Protestant academies of Berlin, Loccum and elsewhere. Moving in those groups of likeminded Muslims and Christians one feels elevated into spheres of paradisical harmony, into a world that could not be better. A newcomer to this symphony might even find it difficult to make out who is who: some blond-haired participants turn out to be Turks and some Germans reveal themselves to be Muslims.

This phenomenon should not be belittled as a dream-world. There is, after all, some chance that this nucleus might develop into a broader movement. Otherwise there would be little hope for European societies of which Islam has become part and parcel. Even if a hundredthousand Turks and other Muslim foreigners are being sent back, the diaspora in France and Germany is going to remain constant at about two million Muslims each. Their isolation can be overcome best by broadening the base of those already existing *crislamic* circles.

Unfortunately this budding Christian-Muslim cooperation is endangered by frequent exploitation for personal, professional, and political ends. Such concomitant trends are undoubtedly human and universal—and, therefore, have to be guarded against. Oddly enough, a fairly large number of Christians and Muslims flock together to form mixed coteries for mutual promotion in the fashionable exercise called dialogue and related activities. Interest groups of experts on matters such as 'integration', 'racial equality', 'Christian-Muslim understanding' etc. tend to devote more energies to self-promotion and the ostracisation of rivals than to the noble cause they purport to advocate. This evokes painful memories of battles among the petty principalities (*taifas*) in decadent Spain: Christians & Muslims versus Christians & Muslims, to the detriment of everyone concerned. Devastating consequences such as the inquisition need not be described here.

Against the background of many an unsavoury distortion and tendentious manipulation of Christian-Muslim cooperation it should not surprise that theology of liberation experiences a resurgence far from the Latin american scene. Catholic and Protestant Students Communities are seeking theological communication with liberation movements from Muslim parts of the Third World. Here the University of Aix-en-Chapelles stands out for its initiatives. Attempts at working toward a 'Christian/ Muslim liberation theology' are, *inter alia*, a counterpoise to the occasional misappropriation of this realm by career hunters. It is a refusal to let interreligious dialogue be monopolised by 'professional partners'. A young generation extremely concerned by the bleak prospects of nuclear war and environmental catastrophies insists on Christian-Muslim cooperation as a necessity. An increasing number of Christians and Muslims even go beyond this and reason that no time should be lost with preliminaries. This was vividly illustrated by the motto of the dialogue meeting at the fringes of the 'Church-Days' in Düsseldorf in 1985: 'The earth belongs to the Lord—Chriatians and Muslims are jointly responsible for this world!' This was also the way Christians and Muslims working together at the academy in Hamburg took the word *Mission* to mean their joint mission in this world.

PART II

Hinduism and Christianity

Bithika Mukerji

Christianity in the Reflection of Hinduism

CHRISTIANITY IN THE REFLECTION OF HINDUISM

The History of the study of alien religious experience in
Judaism, Islam, Hinduism, Buddhism and Confucianism
remains to be written.[1]

SINCE THESE lines were written by Joachim Wach nearly thirty years ago,
no significant contribution has been made in this direction by any of the
religions named by him. Christianity, on the other hand, is distinguished by its
preoccupation with other faiths. From within the region of exclusivity which
he learns to cherish and guard, the Christian is constantly called upon to
address *'the other',* to bring him to a realisation of the need for the saving
grace of Christ. The role of 'the other' therefore, is crucial as the partner in this
on-going process of dialogue, where dialogue is used as the adumbration of
the Christian message.[2]

The Hindu scholar has nothing to show as against the bulk of literature
compiled by Christian missionaries or the stupendous work done by
Indologists. It could be a rewarding undertaking to examine the reasons for
this lack of awareness of alien religions in the reflection of Hinduism, but for
the purpose of this paper one factor alone needs to be stressed as relevant to
the issue. The Hindu, in general, is not called upon to preach his religion to
'the other'. 'The other', to the Hindu is a *fellow-pilgrim* rather as if a mirror
which reflects his own self-understanding. Since evangelisation forms no part
of his own faith he can easily countenance any alternate scheme of worship as
a viable way of religious life. His appreciation for 'the other's' devotional

31

attitude would preclude him from making any belittling criticisms, even in self-defence. That, indeed would be 'anathema' to the Hindu.

The Hindu does not or need not recognise situations of 'challenges' or 'confrontations' in the sphere of commitment to God. He would rather feel called upon to view with utmost sensitivity the *dimension of the sacred being presented to him*. It must be acknowledged however, that ordinarily no such demand is made upon the Hindu by Christians. As far as Christianity is concerned, Hinduism comprises of the entire gamut of heresies from paganism to pantheism and thus the Hindu may be an ideal partner in a dialogue but never the spokesman for a way to God-realisation.

Christianity in the reflection of Hinduism, consequently could be seen only as it presents itself to an alien culture. In order to clarify this, the *first part* of the paper takes up the assessment of the changing order of the role of Christianity with regard to Hinduism. As a complementary thesis, in the *second part* of the paper, an attempt is made to delineate the Hindu meaning of 'revelation'. It is true that Hinduism is not considered to be a revealed religion by Christianity, nevertheless a focussing on its source of inspiration may make it clear how a commonwealth of religions is not only acceptable but rather a matter of celebration to the Hindu. By this separation of issues it is hoped that the possibility of mutual understanding could be envisaged at a deeper level than that of a dialogue.

1. CHRISTIANITY IN CONFRONTATION WITH OTHER TRADITIONS

The long history of Christianity is enriched by the dedicated work of men who devoted themselves to the task of carrying out the commandment:

> All power is given unto me in heaven and in earth. Go ye,
> therefore and teach all nations, baptising them in the
> name of the Father, and of the Son, and of the Holy
> Ghost: teaching them to observe all things what so ever I
> have commanded you: and Go, I am with you always *even*
> unto the end of the world. Amen
>
> (Matt. 28.18)

The *coming of Christ* was the supremely unique event in history which gave a new direction to human destiny. The Cross symbolises the intersection of transcendence and immanence, the vertical descent of the Divine onto the horizontal plane of the mundane. Out of compassion, God chose to participate in the human condition as Man so that men by taking refuge in this act for grace, may overcome death and attain salvation.

The small band of disciples who preached this Gospel to all nations became *the Church of Christ.* All alien religions came into contact with Christianity through the ministry of the Church. Thus the Church is important as the gateway to Christianity. The *movement of evangelisation is* of some interest to the Hindu because thus far his experience of Christianity has had no chance to go beyond it. Hinduism, prepared to revel in its so called 'paganism', was required to view it as a 'defilement'[3]. His most cherished philosophical ideas regarding the unity of the self with Brahman was trivialised as the natural reaction of a tropical people against robust individualism.[4]

More recently, Hinduism has been seen as an ancient culture which can rise to sublime heights of spirituality. In this the case of Hinduism is comparable to Hellenic culture. The Church Fathers had conceded that philosophy is admissible as preparation for the coming of the Church. The same criterion could be applied to Hinduism as well. All ancient cultures have produced or are capable of producing men of outstanding faith who are no doubt moved by the spirit of God, and as such eligible for entry into the Church.

Christianity in confrontation with other traditions, cultures, ways of worship, remained unshaken in its self-confidence as the *unique message* of God for mankind. The combination of faith and dogma cast in the mould of providential eschatology was a powerful force which rode the crest of missionary zeal for many centuries.

The present century has brought about many changes in the outlook of the Church. We live now under the shadow of a crisis situation. This has created a new mood of sensitivity regarding inter-religious confrontations. The movement of *ecumenism* within the Protestant Church as well as the II Vatican Council have brought about an openness toward 'the other' which has radicalised the methodology of conversion.

Hinduism would welcome this change but it is obliged to see that evangelisation lies at the heart of Christianity. Because the acceptance of the authenticity of other religions by the II Vatican Council seems bracketted by the suggestion that the non-Christian multitudes have the right to listen to the Gospels and so the idea of the Christian mission would seem to remain. It is true that a few eminent theologians have sought to minimise the 'otherness' of alien religions. Karl Rahner's theory of Anonymous Christianity has found wide favour in this context. The orthodox Christian, however dismisses it as amounting to an equalisation of all religions and to the Hindu it seems another form of being forced into the matrix of preparedness for the Church.

In truth, the *Hindu* is such a stranger to the concept of an institutionalised religion that he is *unable to appreciate the prescriptive role of the Church.* The Church has a peculiarly singular way as it were of looking at the spiritual map of the world. The totality of the perspective is transfixed to one unique vantage point. If we consider the meaning of the word 'perspective' as used by Shakespeare we can see the implication of the Christian interpretation of human destiny:

> ... perspectivse, which when rightly gazed upon
> Show nothing but confusion; ey'd awry
> Distinguish form. (*Richard Second* II.11.18)

The world, to the Christian, is a jumbled facade which must be 'ey'd awry' through the slant of the New Covenant. He is unable to see meaning or truth in 'the other's' way of worship. In this context we may refer to the famous sermon by Paul which serves as a model for evangelists at all times:

> For as I passed by, and behold your devotions I found an
> altar whith this inscription TO THE UNKNOWN GOD.
> Whom, therefore, ye ignorantly worship, him I declare to
> you. (*Acts* 17.23)

The question may be raised whether the Athenians could have said to Paul: 'Him that you have found now, we already render homage to because he is truly unknown but not unknowable.' We must stretch our imagination further and say that Paul would then have identified the philosophy of the Athenians as the heresy of gnosticism.

This brings us to the second part of the paper. *Hinduism emphasises the 'unknown-ness' of God but not His unknowability.* It is man's privilege, to respond to the highest calling for engaging in the most worthwhile adventure of life. The certainty of success alone is stated by the Hindu scriptures, leaving him free to choose his own way of engaging in this endeavour. All religions have a ritualistic structure of worship. A *wide range of possibilities* seems almost inevitable because men do not react in the same way to the quest for God-realisation. The Hindu scriptures therefore, celebrate the infinite ways of God's participation in human affairs, not seeking to deny that every occasion of the manifestation of his grace is unique in itself.

2. THE AUTHENTICATING OF MANY RELIGIONS IN HINDUISM

Revelation pertains to the unmanifest, the unspoken, the ultimately hidden mystery of existence. The stirring of interest in the meaning of the givenness of the many-splendoured universe is felt within the heart.[5] The Indian scriptures always mention *the heart* in this context possibly because the brain is too ready with resolutions which makes opaque what it seeks to understand. It is not in the nature of reason to await answers. Thus an inwardisation of the questing spirit marks the beginning of an awareness of the longing for penetrating the mystery of existence.

The heart experiences *a yearning for the supreme felicity of a 'home coming'* which is endemic to the human condition itself. It is natural for the traveller, who finds himself out of tune with his surroundings, to seek to return whence he came and where he could be himself. To such a pilgrim the scriptures speak of the final state of self-realisation which is in the nature of a supreme gain.[6]

The nature of this *'supreme gain'* is stated obliquely in many ways, in paradoxes in anecdotes and also in the form of the dialogue between teacher and disciple. The 'Unknown-ness' of the nature of the final finding is not disclosed because in the ultimate analysis the supreme living experience cannot be communicated as a commensurable commodity. It is felt within the being of the aspirant and needs no confirmation because the experience is self-authenticating. The man of enlightenment, thereafter, by his way of being in the world forges another link in the chain of living examplars in the tradition who inspire other pilgrims toward the way of spiritual life.

The man of realisation is *a seer, a sage* who can bear *witness* to the reality of the dimension of the unspoken, but eminently speakable which manifests itself in the unity of soundless resonance and the vision of divine prefiguration of letters known as the *mantra*. The mantra, a pulsating unity of sound and vision, by flashing into the consciousness of the seer, irradiates his understanding so that he is in tune with the cosmic rhythm of the universe. This experiencing of the unveiling of the ultimate mystery is celebrated in the sacred language of *the Vedas*. The Vedas are therefore a celebration of the experience of fulfillment which imparts authenticity to the promise of 'supreme gain'. The language of the Veda itself is of the nature of Truth itself. It is distinguished from secular language by virtue of the particular order of the arrangement of syllables, the sequence of words and the rythm which holds them together. The unity of all three is the mantra.

The Vedic tradition has been preserved by a very exact system of memorising and recitation. The mantra is not created by man and has its being in the enlightened consciousness of the seer, the poet, and thus it perpetuates a living tradition of spiritual quest and its fulfillment.

Much has been written on the nature of this *self-realisation*. For the advaita philosophy it is the knowledge of the unity of the self with Brahman. All other vedantic traditions which comprise the religious framework of Hinduism, reject this position. All religions use the language of God-realisation. The devotional prayers of God-intoxicated men have enriched all the languages of India. In the sphere of religious commitment *no dogma* can operate because

God has infinite ways of disclosing Himself to his devotee. Thus variety is a matter of celebration and rejoicing as evidence of the miriad possibilities of the coming together of man and the Person (the Ista) who is dear to his heart. The wealth of man's outpourings of the heart at the feet of the Lord is truely immeasurable and no limits are sought to be put to channelise them in one direction. No one can legislate for another as to the true image of God because *his images are legion.* All forms are his because he is formless, all auspicious qualities are his because he is the ultimate repository of all magnificence.

This fluidity is anchored on the rock of the nature of spiritual aspiration. The *spiritual journey of a pilgrim* begins when he feels the yearning for a restoring of his fragmented existence in the world or in the language of religion when he engages in a steadfast, onepointed, untrammelled seeking for refuge in God. Times and conditions of human existence keep on changing but the yearning for *penetrating the mystery* of our givenness in the world survives. The living voice of Sruti sustains this questioning, inspires the seeker to become a pilgrim and promises that the quest is not in vain but will be crowned with success. Revelation, therefore, in the Indian context perpetuates the asking of questions promising the worthwhileness of the quest.[7] *The answer remains in the region of grace.* It is the region of mystery which indeed makes spiritual life the greatest adventure of human existence.

The highest truth is preserved in *concealment.* There is no will to truth here or a rationalising or dogmatic faith; what is sought to be preserved is the relevance of yearning toward truth.

Christianity in the reflection of Hinduism is yet *another dimension in which God has disclosed himself* to his People. The commitment to Christ is easily understood by a Hindu who is committed to a particular way of devotion in his own tradition. The nature of commitment demands that it should be exclusive, as well as involve the whole being of the pilgrim in search of spiritual fulfillment. It could be said that the Hindu would believe in a community of committed people which is a free association of friends who come together to celebrate each other's way of seeking God-realisation.[8]

Notes:

1. Joachim Wach *Types of Religious Experience* (Chicago 1972) p. 3 (First published 1951)

2. Philipp Potter 'Christ's Mission and Ours in Today's World' in *International Review of Mission,* 62, No. 246

3. Paul Hacker *Theological Foundation of Evangelization,* (St. Augustin 1983) p. 83

4. George Galloway *The Philosophy of Religion* (Edinburgh 1960) (1914) p. 122

5. *Praśna Upanisad* III.6: *Brhādaranyakopanisad* IV. 4.22 etc

6. He who realizes Brahman attains the highest. With reference to that very fact it has been declared: 'Brahman is Reality, Consciousness, Infinitude; he who realises Him treasured in the cave, in the highest space, even as Brahman the omniscient, fulfills all wants at once.' *Taittīriyopanisad* II.1.1.

7. 'I ask you, of that Being who is to be known only from the *Upanisads,* who definitely projects those (all) beings and withdraws them into Himself, and who is at the sametime transcendent.' *Brhadāranyakopanisad* III.9.26

8. Such a way of communication has already been suggested by many eminent theologians such as Prof. R. Panikkar, Swami Abhishiktānanda and Fr. Bede Griffiths to name a few only.

Paulos Mar Gregorios

The Challenge of Hinduism
What Can Christians Learn From It?

1. THE ATTITUDE OF CHRISTIANS TO THE HINDU WORLD HAS VARIED
   FROM APOSTOLIC TIMES TO OUR DAY.

THE FIRST recorded Christian reactions are probably reflected in the second or third century *Acts of Thomas*[1] and other similar apocryphal Christian writings. They hold the view that the main religion of India is a form of worship of idols and that these idols are demonic. The task of the Christian preaching is to overthrow these gods and bring in the Kingdom of God.

A more sophisticated Christian approach developed with *Augustine of Hippo*, in the early fifth century. Augustine's Epistles 103 and 104 reflect a general attitude towards the Hindu and Greek pagan view that all religions aspire to the same goal by diverse paths. Augustine would agree on the common aspiration for meaning and fulfilment in all religious people; he would qualify his agreement, however, by saying that a common aspiration does not mean that all aspirants reach the same goal. Different pathways— yes, provided they lead in the same direction. In fact, says Augustine, there is only one way. Christ is that way. Any other way would lead astray.

Augustine was generous, however, in accepting the possibility of the salvation of the unbeliever. He says in Epistle 102:

> 'Since we affirm that Christ is the word of God, by whom all things were made, ... under whose rule the whole universe, spiritual and material is ordered ... therefore, from the beginning of the human race, whoever believed in Him and in any way knew Him, and led a pious and just life according to his commandments, was undoubtedly saved by Him, in whatever time and place he may have lived'.

This does not say that all religions are good; it states that people who follow the way of Christ knowingly or unknowingly would be saved by Christ— whether they be Hindu or Jew.

The general image that Christians have of Hinduism is that of an idolatrous polytheism, and in some Roman Catholic assessments of religion, Hinduism occupies a low position. *The Second Vatican Council* has acknowledged that Hinduism is more than mere idolatrous polytheism. The Declaration on the Relation of the Church to Non-Christian Religions positively recognises the philosophical, cultural and religious heritage of Hinduism:

> 'Religions however, that are bound up with an advanced culture have struggled to answer the same questions by means of more refined concepts and a more developed language. Thus in Hinduism, men contemplate the divine mystery and express it through an inexhaustible abundance of myths and through searching philosophical inquiry. They seek freedom from the anguish of our human condition either through ascetical practices or profound meditation or a flight to God with love and trust'.

Even in this generous assessment of Hinduism, there lurks a sense of distance. The order in which the Vatican Declaration treats the various religions is itself significant, 'other religions found everywhere', Hinduism, Buddhism, Islam, Judaism—in ascending degrees of closeness to Christianity, it seems.

The Eastern Orthodox approach to other religions has been no better informed. The great Byzantine scholastic theologian *John of Damascus* (ca. 675- ca. 749), was the civil head of the Christian community in the Muslim Caliphate, and left that job because of a conflict with Islam. The Damascene approach to other religions was also largely negative. In the Middle East there were few positive Christian affirmations of other religions until Metropolitan *George Khodr of Lebanon* in our time, whose developed Arab Christian self-awareness was helped by sympathetic Christian Islamicists like the Anglican Kenneth Cragg. Generally speaking Eastern Orthodox appreciation of Hinduism has been very minimal.

Among Catholic approaches to Hinduism special mention should be made of Jules Monchanin, Abhishiktananda, Raymundo Panikkar and Bede Griffiths, who have beaten a path to the very heart of Hindu spirituality. Griffiths has produced several appreciative Christian accounts of Hinduism like *The Golden String* (1954), *Christ in India* (1966), *Return to the Centre* (1976) and *The Marriage of East and West* (1982).

On the *Protestant* side, recent writers are just getting over the *Barth-*

Kraemer rejection of all religion as opposed to the gospel. This was the spirit of the children of Israel, who had been taught by Yahveh to reject and destroy the pagan religions of Palestine and to overthrow their idols. It was also the view of the Jewish Rabbi Saul even as of Paul the Christian Apostle.[2] Calvin and Luther basically followed this early Paul. None of these had the opportunity for direct contact with Hinduism. But even people like Karl Barth, Hendrik Kraemer and Emil Brunner, who could have known something about Hindu faith and thought had they so desired, *followed the Semitic tradition of rejecting other religions without knowing them.*

More recently the idea gained ground in Protestant circles that *secularisation* as a social-cultural process would wipe out the other religions, and that they were irrelevant. The more Catholic view that there is a universal revelation to humanity as a whole, and that other religions may find their source in the Logos who illumines every human person,[3] or the idea of the Noachic Covenant with all humanity found little support in Protestant theological circles. The hope was that if the Christian mission did not wipe out Hinduism, secularisation would. And so there was little need to bother about other religions.

Today, of course, there is a sense of alarm, or at least disquiet, that *European and American young people* are taking to bits and pieces of Hinduism and Buddhism with an avid passion. On the one hand the young people feel that Christianity does not give them the inner peace they need, and that these religions do. On the other hand, there is a recrudescence of ancient European paganism, a revival of cruder forms of neoplatonism and pythagoreanism in Europe. Non-Christian Greeks like Philostratus (died ca 225) wrote treatises like *Apollonius of Tyana* to prove that Hindu, Buddhist and Greek pagans had a better understanding of God than Christians. This attitude is back in the West. In the third century, this was a reaction to the extremism of Christian apologists like Aristides (second century) of Athens, who affirmed the superiority of Christianity over other religions without sufficient knowledge of the latter.

There has been too much uninformed denigration of Hinduism on the part of Christians and it is precisely this that poses the challenge to us to make a greater effort to understand and appreciate whatever is culturally, intellectually and spiritually valuable in Hinduism. We have to move beyond Aristides.

2. THREE FUNDAMENTAL ASPECTS OF HINDUISM

For Christians, in coming to terms afresh with Hindu thought and practice, it is necessary first of all to become aware of the enormous range of variety in Hinduism—perhaps unparalleled in that range by any other religion including Christianity. It would be a mistake to assume that Hinduism is the non-dualism of Sankara. That certainly is a dominant strain in Hinduism, just as Thomism was in Christianity in our century.

It may be difficult for the Christian to do justice to the wide variety within Hinduism; they can, however, recognise three main trends—the Vedic tradition, the Gita-Bhakti Tradition and the Advaita Tradition.

(a) The Vedic Tradition

Personally, for the present writer, the Vedic tradition is by far the most attractive. Unlike the Advaita tradition with its high philosophical sharpness, the Vedic tradition places more emphasis on cosmic and social harmony than on personal salvation *(mukti)* or fulfilment. And for the Vedic world, ritual and sacrifice are more important than thought and understanding. The ablest modern Christian defender of this tradition is beyond doubt Raymundo Panikkar, whose *The Vedic Experience*[4] is fast becoming a classic anthology of the Vedic texts. The centre of the Vedas, according to Panikkar, lies in the perception and practice of *Yajna* or sacrifice which is at the heart of the cosmic order. As the Rg Veda puts it.[5]

'Sacrifice is the navel of the world'

(*Yajno bhuvanasya nabhih*)

The early Vedic tradition related *yajna* (sacrifice) very closely with *rta* (cosmic order). This cosmic order is not a manmade natural law, but the dynamic pulse of the universe; it is upset by human sin and restored and upheld by human *yajna* or sacrificial rite in which gods and men co-operate to sustain and maintain the universe and its cosmic harmony.

Strangely enough, this view has a parallel in the pre-Christian Jewish Rabbinical tradition, where the sacrificial altar of the Jerusalem temple, regarded as indentical with the place where Abraham sought to offer Isaac as a sacrifice, was regarded as the centre of the universe. The rabbinical understanding of sacrifice had much in common with the Vedic concept of sacrifice—a similarity that could be further studied and documented.

Those of us Christians who place the liturgical tradition of worship at a higher level than thought and action find here something extremely attractive. For us Eastern Christians, for example, liturgy and the eucharistic sacrifice express more adequately the meaning of Christ's incarnate mission than theology or ethics ever can.

But sacrifice is more than mere ritual or liturgy as the children of the Enlightment understand these. The Vedas say 'sacrifice is the human person'.

It is human to give of oneself which is true sacrifice. Christ's humanity was best expressed in his self-giving sacrifice. In self-giving a human person becomes himself or herself—this aspect of the Vedic teaching should be a challenge to all Christians.

It is also interesting that the Vedas do not focus always on personal salvation, but put the welfare of the person in the context of the health of the whole. Some forms of Christianity as well as Advaitic thought in Hinduism have been corrupted by too great a pre-occupation with the salvation of the individual; the cost has been a declining care for the whole—for the whole communion of saints, for the whole of humanity, for the whole creation. There is much here for Christians to learn from the Vedas.

(b) The Bhakti Tradition and the Gita

This is perhaps the best and most living aspect of traditional Hindu spirituality. There are so many schools of Bhakti in one form or another. The Bhagavad Gita is the centre of this tradition, but the ancient *Saiva Siddhanta* and the Vaishnavite tradition in general belong to the Bhakti Marga (way). Here too dogma or discursive philosophy is not central. Theology is ancillary to spirituality. And it is right in the midst of life that truth is revealed—in the battlefield, in a chariot already moving—not in the forest or in the meditation chamber.

To take the *Gita* as the central example of the Bhakti tradition is itself a venture open to misunderstanding—for the *Gita's* central message is not devotion but action of a special kind. Sri Aurobindo, one of the best modern interpreters of the *Gita* warns us on this point—against taking devotion as its central point, or self-less action as its essence. According to Aurobindo, this is the summary of *Gita* teaching:

> 'Reposing one's mind and understanding, heart and will
> in Him, with self-knowledge, with God-knowledge, with
> world-knowledge, with a perfect equanimity, a perfect
> devotion, an absolute self-giving, one has to do works as
> an offering to the Master of all self-emergence and all
> sacrifice. Identified in will, conscious with that
> consciousness, That shall decide and initiate the action.[6]

If we substitute the word 'Christ' for 'That' for the present writer, Aurobindo's statement becomes theologically not only acceptable, but much more faithful to the Christian tradition than the theological utterances one hears these days. The *Gita* represents a very dynamic combination of the disciplines of reflection, meditation, devotion and sacrificial unself-regarding action. Knowledge and devotion are not repudiated, but made ancillary to union with the divine and to action inspired by the Spirit. My understanding of Christianity coincides with Sri Aurobindo's summary of the *Gita*, except for the fact that the latter has no reference to the person and work of Christ. But in the *Gita* I find an understanding of life and world and self which for me at least far surpasses that of many modern Christian theologies.

The way of the *Gita* is quite different from the way of classical Vedanta, says Sri Aurobindo. The ultimate Reality with which union is sought is not impersonal, not aloof and austere, not a mere relationless Absolute as in the Vedanta. He or It is both absolute and relational—the transcendent Lord who is the loving and adorable Master. And the realisation of unity with him does not absolve one from all interest in the reality around us. Indwelling in the Master, the Master indwelling the devotee—that is the teaching of the *Gita*— very close to the Christian gospel's 'Abide in me and I in you'. The unity of Soul with the Supreme Self is both in essence of being and in knowledge and bliss—as in Eastern Christianity. 'Thou shalt abide in Me alone' *(nivasishyasi mayyēva)* is a saying of the *Gita*. And of course, as in Eastern Christianity, the process leads to divinisation of *theosis (madbhāvam āgatāh),* being united in nature with the divine-human (sādharmyam āgatāh). One becomes divine *(Brahma-bhūta).*

Christians, with a half-kr owledge of Christian teaching and less knowledge of Hindu teaching, can so quickly dismiss Hinduism either as irrelevant or idolatrous. Which makes me nervous. I wonder about the sincerity of such Christians; for it is a kind of unwillingness to know, which cannot be associated with sincerity, but only with spiritual insecurity or cultural arrogance.

The Bhakti tradition is much wider than the *Gita*, but the challenge of Hinduism at its best to Christianity comes more from the *Gita* tradition than any other, with the exception perhaps of the Vedic.

(c) The Advaitic Tradition

Mis-interpretations by Christians of the *advaita* or non-dualist tradition of Hinduism are widely prevalent. Some Christians have expressed a preference for *Ramanuja's qualified non-dualism (viśishtādvaita),* since they consider it closer to Christian theism than Sankara's absolute non-dualism.

The issue at stake, in Christian terms, is the relation between the Creator and the creation, in Hindu terms Brahman and *jagad* (world). For Ramanuja, the world with human beings as part of that world, is related to Brahman as predicate and subject, as qualities and substance, as body and soul. Brahman creates the world by expanding itself (*pralaya*) and withdraws it (*vilaya*) by condensing it into itself. Brahman can be related to persons through love and devotion in *Viśishtādvaita*.

For *Sankara* on the other hand all personal relations and worship belong to the non-knowing (*avidya*) state, though not to be condemned on that account. For worship and devotion, with disciplined meditation (*manana*), are the way to transcending all dualist knowledge (*apará-vidya*) in the final realisation (*siddhi*), where the separation between known, knower and knowledge (*jnēya*, *jnātā* and *jnāna*) is overcome.

The world itself for Sankara, is not an entity existing in itself; it is a projection of Brahman, apprehended in human nescience as something apart from oneself and from the Brahman. It is caused by the concealing (*āvarana sākti*) and projecting *(vikshēpasakti)* powers of Brahman[7] in combination with the subject-object non-knowledge of the unrealised human soul. Once the true knowledge of the Brahman and oneself is attained, all duality falls away. It becomes a matter of first-hand experience that the self *(jīva)*, God *(Brahman)* and world *(jagad)* are not three separate realities, but only different manifestations under certain conditions of the same one reality.

The claim of the non-dualist philosphy is not that this can be logically demonstrated. Sankarites claim that the affirmation of non-duality comes from the absolute experience and not from discursive thought. So no rational argument against the affirmation can have any special validity.

But are *Christians* justified in dismissing all this as but a specious argument? I think not. Because the argument for the distinction between Creator and the Creation in traditional Christian theism is also full of rational difficulties. If theism argues for an infinite God, then the Creation cannot be something outside of that God, as a separate entity. For the infinite cannot have an outside, since it has no boundaries. Logically theists will have to acknowledge some form of pan-en-theism, since anything and everything can only be inside an infinite God and not outside it. There cannot be a God plus Creation if God is infinite. How can there be infinity *plus* something else? Theists have to acknowledge that God and world are not two. In essence this is also what Sankarite non-dualism says, though Christian theists would not want to affirm the absolute identity of Self, World and God as the Sankarite says.

But *Hindu non-dualism* gets some *confirmation from two other sources.* First, in the Christian *mystical tradition* also there is the experience-based affirmation that all duality disappears in the mystical experience. As in Advaita, this is not a logical argument, but a first-hand experience of the mystic which cannot be logically transmitted. Secondly, the insights into the nature of reality gained by contemporary *physical theory* also affirm the total integral relation of the Cosmos and the basic non-duality of the whole. The holistic or holographic understanding of the universe supports the non-dualist approach to reality.

Christian theologians have even in recent times been guilty of affirming the absolute qualitative otherness of the Divine, thus placing humanity and world as totally other to God. If humanity and world were to be totally other to God or outside God, then we will have to affirm a finite God and a finite universe outside God—leading to a dualism that can hardly be philosophically respectable.

The challenge of Hinduism is basically a call to Christians to enter into respectful dialogue. Again, it is a matter of experience that such dialogue, sincerely and humbly undertaken, leads to deepening of the Christian's understanding of Christ and of reality.

Notes

1. *Periodoi Thoma.* There are many other texts of Egyptian or Syrian provenance which speak of Hindus. For example the non-Christian Hermetic Coptic Text *Asclepius* 21-29 (VI:71) speaks of Hindus along with Scythians as 'Barbarians'.

2. *Romans* 1:19, *Acts* 14: 15-17, 17: 22-31

3. *John* 1:4, 9

4. London, 1977

5. I: 164

6. Sri Aurobindo *Essays on the Gita* (Pondicherry 1972) p. 34

7. The concept of *māya*, which is central to Sankara's thought is often mis-interpreted as meaning falsehood or illusion. This is not the case. Sankara makes a clear distinction between the absolute level of truth *(paramārthika satta)* and the operational or practical level *Vyāvahārika-Salta).* *Māya* is the duality that appears at the practical commonsense level of perception. When the true identity of *Brahman, atman* (soul) and *jagad* (world) is realised in the higher experience of absolute truth, then all separation is understood as mere projection and not as ultimate reality.

Michael von Brück

Collaboration between Christians and Hindus (The Example of India)

1. INDIAN CHRISTIANITY AND SOCIO-ECONOMIC STRUCTURES

CHRISTIANS AND Hindus work together daily in their millions in the economic and other sectors of Indian society. Yet a conscious collaboration towards some common aim or concern is rare. Hindus and Christians are unequal partners, and this goes for their sociological and demographic as well as their culturo-spiritual self understanding. Whereas some 83 per cent of the population of India counts as Hindu, only 2.6 per cent declare themselves to be Christian. These few Christians are concentrated in defined regions, particularly the North-Eastern states (Nagaland, Mizoram, Meghalaya), Kerala and the Kanyakumari-District of Tamil Nadu. Round about 80 per cent of Christians belong to the lower castes, are casteless or aboriginal, and so, quite apart from their religion, are scarcely dialogue partners for the upper and culture-bearing castes of the Hindus. What is more, Christianity is felt to be a *foreign body* introduced artificially into India by the colonial powers. This had the result that with the flowering of nationalism which followed independence Christians took on the burden of proving themselves to be loyal citizens. These are all factors that contributed to Christians in very large measure being cut off from the mainstream of society. They often have identity problems.

The *Syrian-Orthodox Christians* alone enjoy an independent Indian tradition. They claim to go back to the apostle Thomas but have at any rate certainly been settled above all along the Malabar coast since the fourth century. They constitute a caste of their own that is generally acknowledged and is of relatively high standing. Relationships between them and the Hindus in Kerala are friendly because the Orthodox neither proselytise nor question the Hindu caste system. On account of the vicissitudes of their history and the hundreds years, long attempt of Roman Catholic missionaries to submit them to papal jurisdiction they are so split among themselves that every now and then Hindu groups simply pick them off.

The Roman Catholic mission since the sixteenth century and the Protestant missions since the eighteenth have been closely bound up with European colonial history. The converts often bowed to the political and economic pressure of the conquerors. This is why in the eyes of traditional Hindus they appeared to be more or less traitors. This also goes largely for the Muslims. But since Christians were granted educational privileges and more schools of higher education were built by Englishmen and until 1947 remained virtually in their hands, Christianity exercises an influence quite disproportionate to its size. Secular India today for the most part acknowledges positively the important contribution *Christian schools* and colleges—and hospitals— continue to make. According to the constitution independent India counts as a secular State, i.e. there is no established religion, as in the neighbouring kingdom of Nepal, in which Hinduism is declared to be the religion of the State and baptism is made an imprisonable offence. The Indian State guarantees freedom of religion, and this includes the right to confess, practise and proclaim whatever religion one has.

The European mission was most successful among the groups which were not integrated into the Hindu caste system, that is to say above all the casteless and the aboriginal tribes. Often enough such people converted not for material advantages but simply to be recognised as human beings, that is to say, to attain that basic human dignity that Hindu society had for thousands of years denied them. But because the Christian churches could not overcome the caste system, these groups nowadays tend to convert to Islam or Buddhism (Ambedkars neo-Buddhism). Conversion has become a political weapon on the part of some ninety million casteless people in their struggle for social emancipation.

Hinduism is tolerant and does not lay down any confession of faith. A Hindu is one who belongs to a caste and keeps the rules of caste within and outside the caste. A convert knowingly breaks out of this system and is liable to fall foul of the anger of the caste. While radical groups (the Dalit movement) call for a war against caste, most Christians try to find a specific identity outside the social conflicts of Hindu society. While the government maintains a special programme for the promotion of the registered lower castes (the casteless and the aboriginal tribes), by reserving places for education and employment, Christians are often caught in a rending ordeal: they are excluded from the application of these measures since they are officially outside the caste system.

An interesting development over the past ten years is the founding of associations (*sabha*) by certain castes which comprise all members of similar castes regardless of their religious affiliation. These groups are becoming stronger especially in the middle range of castes (Nadars in Tamil Nadu, and so on), and in them Hindus and Christians of the same caste work together for economic and political aims that emerged out of the modernisation of India (common political platforms): caste loyalty is stronger than religious affiliation despite the hundreds of years of efforts of the missionaries in a contrary sense.

Anybody who wants to track down, rightly assess and promote attempts at collabration between Hindus and Christians must be mindful of this background. The religious problem cannot be separated from socio-economic structures in India any more than elsewhere.

2. TOWARDS A HISTORY OF COLLABORATION

The first deliberate attempts at collaboration were made by the Portuguese Jesuit missionary *Roberto de Nobili* (1577-1656). He came to India in 1606 and worked above all in the region of Madurai. He soon realised that it was necessary to bring the Brahmin leaders of culture nearer the gospel. This is why he wanted to become a brother to the Brahmins, that is to say, he became a strict vegetarian, wore the *dhoti* instead of European trousers, imitated with unspeakable hardships the life style of the wandering ascetics (sannyāsin) and learned Sanskrit and Tamil above all. He learned both languages to perfection to the point that the indigenous élites paid him the highest respect. In his adaptation to the Indian life-style he went so far as to accept the caste system and even untouchability, something that earned him bitter criticism from his Jesuit confrères. Thus it is with de Nobili that we find the first determined effort to inculturate Christianity, and yet we have to be clear about his motivation: he was concerned to convert Hindus to the Catholic Church. It is not yet possible to speak of a spirit of collaborative partnership. To this day Hindus have never forgotten this and that is why very often they remain sceptical about Christian efforts to bring the gospel closer to Indians by means of Indian philosophy, art and rites, where they do not outright repudiate them. They do not trust the motivation.

The beginnings of collaboration are to be discerned in the German

Lutheran *Bartholomäus Ziegenbalg* (1683-1719). Under Danish protection—though in practice on the side of the Indians against the Danish military authorities—he built up his mission in Tranquebar, collected the treasury of Tamil literature and in 1712 composed the first Tamil dictionary. He had Tamil school-books printed for elementary schools and thereby laid the foundation-stone for a far-reaching educational effort in South India. Here too, naturally, the aim was finally to bring the pupils to conversion.

There can be no overestimating the importance of the research into native languages that Christian linguists undertook. The *Hindu renaissance* of the nineteenth century was perhaps unthinkable without the work of leading Sanskritists like Max Müller. Even today this is not forgotten and the research into Sanskrit and other literatures that is undertaken together forms one of the most important starting-points for collaboration between Hindus and Christians, at least in the cultural field.

This renaissance reached a high point in the *Brahmo Samaj* founded by *Raja Mohan Roy* in 1830. Under the impact of the spiritual greatness of Jesus of Nazareth, who could be honoured in India as one of the many incarnations of the one godhead, and of the social charitable works of the Christian missionaries those around him wanted to renew Hinduism as a way of life with clearly humanistic aims by seeing it as a montheism that had gone to school with the Vedānta and the Sermon on the Mount. Pluralism of religions, peace between them and cooperation were the concepts of an enlightened Hindu spirituality which also sought to cut out the excrescences of the caste system as well as to root out the polytheistic tendencies of popular Hinduism. The third leader of the *Brahmo Samaj, Keshab Chander Sen,* was particularly influenced by the Bible. What came about was an inner exchange of religions, even on occasion a cooperation between the Samaj and many individual missionaries, but scarcely a broadly-based phase of dialogue between official Christianity and intellectuals (who were for the most part Bengalis).

It was in this way that *Dayananda Sarasvati* in 1875 founded *Arya Samaj,* which propagated a return to the Vedas and a clear demarcation from Christianity. They went so far as to introduce a rite for the reconversion to Hinduism. This movement on occasions became aggressive; this was a reaction against the claim of the Christian churches to be the sole preachers of truth.

In the encounter between Hindus and Christians the figure of *Ramakrishna* (1836-1886) stands out, and he still exercises a world-wide influence through the Ramakrishna-mission founded by *Vivekenanda* in 1897. During his deepest trances Ramakrishna was so completely sunk in the godhead that he could perfectly see the form of God (*murti*) he meditated from time to time.

He also had a vision of Christ, which became decisive for the attitude of many Hindus towards Christianity: Jesus appeared as an Oriental, one of the greatest spiritual masters of all time, who was rightly named God. Europeans had interpreted him falsely and misused him as a tool of an imperialistic mission. In Ramakrishna's own words: 'The Saviour is the messenger of God. He is like the viceroy of a mighty king. When there are disturbances in a far-away province, the king sends his viceroy to settle them. This is the way God sends his saviour whenever religion goes under anywhere in the world. It is always the one and the same saviour, born out of the ocean of life, who springs up in one place and is called Krishna, then sinks down in order to spring up again in another place as Christ.' So far as its practical form is concerned, the Ramakrishna mission is greatly influenced by the Christian religious orders. It promotes education and practises works of mercy.

3. CHRISTIAN ASHRAMS

During the last thirty years, and especially since Vactican II and through the corresponding programme of the World Council of Churches a new spirit has been introduced in to the exchanges between Hindus and Christians under the slogan 'Dialogue'. In this time there have been more or less regular official theological dialogues on a dogmatic level, which put up interesting material for discussion and are meant to serve mutual understanding and dismantle prejudices. Not infrequently these meetings degenerate into monologues which become self-exhibitions. At best people talk to each other, but they are not always inclined really to listen to each other. This is why a certain disenchantment set in during the seventies, which goes to explain the decline in the number of dialogue groups (usually gathered by a Christian initiator sympathetic to dialogue and only seldom systematically forwarded—as by the Hindu Divine Life Society in the Shivananda Ashram) as well as of the larger-scale conferences in the towns.

Dialogue has to be anchored in the 'depths of the heart', that is to say, in shared prayer, in meditation and silence. This was something that was seen early by a few Indian and foreign Christians who wanted to latch on to the life-style of an Indian ashram. The ashram is a community that outwardly is relatively unorganised and is made up of a spiritual master and his pupils, who spontaneously flock round him. People live materially undemanding lives and in prayer. Anybody who comes is a member of the community, anybody who goes needs no permission to do so. Today there are more than forty *Christian ashrams,* which are places of spiritual meeting or work in common between

Hindus and Christians. Two examples: the first Christian ashram (Christikulu Ashram) was founded by an Indian and a British doctor in 1921 in the neighbourhood of Tiruppatur in South India. It was a place of meeting and of common service of the sick. Gandhi visited it. *J. Monchanin* (who died in 1957) and *H. le Saux* (Swami Abhishiktananda, who died in 1973) founded a stable contemplative ashram completely in the Indian tradition in Shantivanam, near Tiruchipalli (1950). In 1968 Abhishiktandanda went as hermit to the Himalayas in order to live a life of yoga and undisturbed meditation which brought him to the centre of the Indian experience of non-duality (*advaita*). Many Hindu-Christian groups have gathered in his memory and tradition. Today the ashram has under the leadership of the Benedictine monk *Bede Griffiths* become a centre of dialogue between the religions, the New Age and the Church, science and belief. Impulses go out from here to the whole world—less so perhaps into the immediate village neighbourhood. For the inhabitants of the Indian village live under the caste system and scarcely cultivate (religious) contact with other castes. Since caste inherently means religion, dialogue necessarily involved cooperation between different castes, which is still difficult for socio-psychological as well as political reasons, and this is the reason why it has remained an important concern for intellectuals and quite especially for contemplatives from all traditions.

4. SOCIAL ACTION GROUPS

This phenomenon deserves great attention since about twelve thousand social action groups have come into being spontaneously since around 1960. These groups are conducted for the most part by young people. They may come from any religious background but often they emphatically repudiate this ('all religions increase misery'), or else they want to use it in the service of a struggle for social emancipation like an inter-religious liberation theology. It can, however, happen that such groups ground themselves in common prayer, which leaves behind the usual religious restrictions. Their aim is to awaken a new consciousness among the masses of India as well as to organise people into unions or cooperatives. But since groups are quite often suspected of Marxism by both the churches and the Hindu establishment, they tend to drift away from the mainstream of the religious traditions. A few small colleges enter into dialogue with them or organise conferences at which such groups can meet representatives of the leading élite of Hinduism. Whether a fruitful cooperation can develop out of this remains to be seen.

To sum up, one can say that collaboration between Hindus and Christians is of vital importance, although the difficulties often still seem to be insuperable. Then political problems (the Tyagi bill to restrict conversions), the not unjustifiable mistrust on the part of Hindus, especially by reason of the financial dependence of the churches in India on foreign missionary societies, which continue to organise crusades for conversion, and the lack of continuity in the work of dialogue at every level make the collaboration between Hindus and Christians considerably difficult.

PART III

Buddhism and Christianity

Sulak Sivaraksa

Christianity in the Reflection of Buddhism

1. BUDDHIST TOLERANCE-CHRISTIAN INTOLERANCE

WHEN THE first missionary went to Tibet to propagate the gospel, the Tibetan Buddhist monks heard about God, Salvation, Liberation, Suffering, Eternal Life and the like. They concluded that the teaching of Christ was similar to that of the Buddha.

The *strength and weakness of Buddhism* is that it tends *to find similarity with other religions.* Hence it finds no difficulty in coexisting with Hinduism and Animism. The differences are not stressed. The argument is that for the majority, if they find any religious rites and rituals helpful to them, they should practice them. For instance, Shrines, Images and Gods could be refuges to those who are in need of spiritual protection or security, at least temporarily. Once one develops oneself more maturely, one will have inner strength to solve one's own difficulty, to be really one with oneself, as well as with all beings and with the ultimate reality. For those who wish to develop further towards Selflessness in order to get to the state of Oneness or Nothingness, then they can take the Buddha's Middle Path seriously. Yet Buddhism does not claim that it is the only one that knows the answer to the problem of suffering and how to overcome it—to reach the final Liberation or Nirvāna.

Unlike Hindus, the *Christians found it difficult to admit that Buddhism could also be a true religion.* The missionary in Tibet told the Lama frankly that Buddhism was a false religion or the religion of the demons, and only by following Jesus Christ one could be saved or attain a blissful state of the eternal life.

Unfortunately this kind of belief is still wide spread in many Christian circles. Despite Vatican Council II, some documents from the Secretariat for the non-Christian still make many Buddhists believe that the official Vatican policy towards Buddhism is still not clear. There is an implication that now Christians should learn more about Buddhism and show outward sign of respect of Buddhist ceremony in order to understand Buddhist teaching and culture, which will perhaps make it easier to convert Buddhists to Christianity, or to christianise Buddhism as St. Thomas Aquinas had christianised Aristotle.

At least in Siam, the leading Catholic seminary still publishes articles saying that the Buddha was at best is a prophet, pointing the way to Jesus Christ, or that Buddhism was dead historically as soon as Christ was born 543 years after the Buddha had passed away.

This kind of assertion or accusation may annoy many uneducated Buddhists. But for those who practise Buddhism seriously, they take no interest in ignorant utterances from anyone; why should one quarel over misunderstanding or propaganda? Indeed there are so many lofty ideas in Christianity that Buddhism could reflect upon.

2.   GOD IN BUDDHISM?

God is obviously the utmost important issue in Christianity. If the Buddhists look at the word God unsympathetically, they will automatically deny his existence. They may even go further as to say that blind faith in the Unknown which equates to the Ultimate Reality is in fact Ignorance (*Avijja*)—the root cause of all evils. Especially the idea of God the Father, through human history in his begotten Son, would be beyond any Buddhist imagination not to mention the Holy Spirit, or the doctrine of the Trinity.

At best the Buddhists will say *God as expressed in Christianity has no role in Buddhism.* We are not interested in monotheism, polytheism or atheism. Yet, Buddhism is *not agnosticism.* If the Buddhists are concerned about the ultimate reality or Noble Truth (*Ariya sacca*) the righteous law which controls or operates the Universe (*Sada dhamma*) which means that whatever one does, one will reap the fruit of one's action (*Kamma*), then we must reflect upon this in the light of the Christian concept of God also.

The Christians explain about God from the Hebraic historical perspective of a tribe, so God became so personal to them. He was even conceived as a God of anger. This was purely human interpretation. Only in the New Testament could we conceive *him* as the God of love, and he was for all mankind—beyond the Jewish people. As Meister Ekhardt said, any definition or understanding of God is bound to fail, unless you have experienced him.

In Buddhism, we could not explain or define *Nirvāna either*. We can give some negative indications that *Nirvāna* is not this, is not that, and we can give some positive indications that *Nirvāna* is the perfect state of peace and happiness. Yet it is also a state beyond happiness.

3. THE BUDDHA AND THE CHRIST

When Gautama became Buddha, he was *enlightened*. Although he still remained man, he already united with the Ultimate Reality-God, so the Buddha is God—not in the personification sense but in a normative sense. Hence the ultimate reality in Buddhism is Buddha Dhamma—not merely Dhamma in the traditional Brahministic sense of the word. Indeed in the Mahayana tradition, the concept of Adi Buddha or Dyani Buddha is really the creator of the universe and the universal law.

From the Buddhist perspective, Sakayamuni Buddha or *Gautama Buddha* is the only one which could be *verified* by history as we understand it, for he was born about the sixth to the seventh centuries B.C. *Other Buddhas* before him could *not be verified* by history and Dyani Buddha is even beyond history. Is Dyani Buddha a myth or a reality? Only those who are enlightened or those with religious experience with God or Buddha Dhamma could really answer this.

Venerable Buddhadas Bhikkhu, a well known Thai monk, helps us, who have no religious experience, to understand this problem by pointing out that in any religion, Buddhism included, there are always *two kinds of language*: (1) the religious or Dhammic language and (2) the ordinary or worldly language.

We tend to mix these two kinds of language and make so much misunderstanding unnecessarily. If the Christians hear that the Buddhists claim that their *Buddha equals to the Christian God*, they become angry. The Buddhist likewise feels that his Buddha must be superior to Jesus Christ. This is childish and tribal; it is a missuse of Dhammic language. In fact there is no equality nor superiority or inferiority among different religions. We are different but we ought to respect the others and try to understand the essential concept of our friends' religion as sympathetically and as respectfully as we can. Even so, we may make mistakes. Then we should ask forgiveness too.

4. SUFFERING, SALVATION, LIBERATION

It is difficult enough to understand our own religion clearly and thoroughly. Yet in this day and age, we must admit the *limitation of our own religious tradition, and try to understand other religions* in the light of our understanding of our own religion. A Buddhist could only reflect on Christianity from a Buddhist perspective, he could do no more. If the Buddhists understand that the Christian love of God makes him love his neighbours, his submission to God makes him selfless and is compassionate to all beings—human or other wise, (like St. Francis of Assisi for instance), his understanding will make him reflect that to him the Buddha is indeed the Compassionate One and the Enlightened One. If he followed in the Buddha's footsteps, he could understand himself and the society as well as the natural phenomena around him. His understanding in fact arises from his non exploitation of himself and others. The more selfless he is, the more compassionate.

The more he sees that others are *suffering*, the more he would like to share their suffering and together with them to eliminate the cause of suffering. By doing so, he takes a Bodhisattva vow to be compassionate like the past Buddhas or the Buddha-to-be.

If he has encounters with Christianity, he sees *the cross* as a sign that will strengthen him to share suffering—not only with his Christian friends but also with all God's creatures. Being a Buddhist, he will want to find the cause of suffering in order to get rid of it for his own liberation as well as the liberation of all others.

When the Buddhist reflects on Christian teaching or suffering, salvation and liberation, he finds all these meaningful from his Buddhist context. His Christian friends may seek salvation through Jesus Christ, but being Buddhist he finds Christ's teaching, especially the sermon on the Mount, and Christ's lively readiness to obey God the Father and serving God's people very meaningful. This meaning he gets through his understanding of the Dhammic language, which is obviously different from the Orthodox Christian interpretation. The Buddhist therefore feels that once a Christian fulfils his duty by firmly believing in God as he understands him and acts according to God's commandments by loving his neighbours, sharing suffering with them and try to overcome the cause of that suffering, he will surely be liberated. For the Buddhist that state of liberation will be without hatred, greed and delusion—in other words it is a state of *enlightenment*.

The Christian may call this an *eternal life*. The Buddhist would not quarrel with the use of terminology, whether there is a permanent soul or not is left to the worldly language to tackle. If eternal life means perfect happiness, beyond word or description, it may also mean *Nirvāna*.

This is my personal reflection which is not scholarly. We need more serious research than an article of this nature can achieve in order to develop deeply into the Buddhist reflection on Christianity—a fascinating subject.

Aloysius Pieris

Buddhism as a Challenge for Christians

1. BUDDHIST CHALLENGE NEUTRALISED

MANY HAD hoped with Arnold Toynbee that an in-depth encounter between Buddhism and Christianity would usher in a new era in human history. For these two religions are a formidable challenge to each other as no two other religions are, and their encounter, one hopes, would result in a *coincidentia oppositorum* giving birth to a richer and nobler synthesis in each.

The actual events, however, have belied these expectations because these two religions have never met each other in their *authentic* forms except perhaps in the hearts of a few individuals. It was often a case of a deformed Christianity colliding with a misapprehended Buddhism. The ideology of 'Euro-Ecclesiastical Expansionism' which claimed to be the religion of Christ was not Good News but a serious threat to Buddhism. In fact, it was this initial Christian offensive that compelled the Buddhists to wear a *defensive mask* when facing the Christians. This mask is still on.

A hardening of positions took place in the nineteenth century when a bitter controversy broke out between English Christianity and Sinhalese Buddhism: a Christianity which was occupying a politically advantageous position in a Buddhist culture in Asia but was insecure in Europe in the prevailing climate of scientific rationalism and secular ideologies; and a Buddhism which was trying to retrieve its rightful place in a colonised nation and to vindicate its intellectual respectability in Europe by *presenting itself as a 'religion-less' philosophy having a scientific and rationalist basis.*[1]

This was the beginning of what one Buddhist sociologist has described as

Protestant Buddhism, i.e. a Buddhism originating as a protest against an unchristian Christianity which was aggressive and contemptuous towards the doctrine and the person of Buddha.[2] This reaction continued up to the middle of our own century in the guise of a 'modernist Buddhism' apologetical in style and content.[3] For it would not hesitate to employ such philosophical labels as 'rationalism', 'empiricism', and even 'logical positivism' for the purpose of interpreting the Buddha's spiritual message to the West.

This kind of *'Export Buddhism'* (to borrow a phrase from Edward Conze), though widespread now, failed to be what it was meant to be: a challenge to Christians. For, it was just a dry doctrinal system with no religious sap to make it live, with no monastic nucleus to nourish it spiritually, and with no Buddha-cultus to symbolise its essentially soteriological character. This nineteenth century legacy still continues to hinder Christians from detecting what is truly challenging in Buddhism.

Though the polemical climate has yielded place to a friendly atmosphere of dialogue, the last century's doctrinaire approach to Buddhism still persists in the works of most theologians. David Snellgrove's sophisticated tract on the 'theology of Buddahood' is an example.[4] Recently, John Cobb and George Rupp have been hailed as two Christians who have allowed their theology to be revolutionised by the Buddhist challenge to Christian thought.[5] Though an intellectually fascinating exercise, a confrontation of Whitehead's process philosophy with the subtleties of ancient Buddhist dialecticians like Nagarjuna (Cobb does it brilliantly) is a far cry from an encounter between the gospel and the Dharma!

The Asian theologians have been even less enterprising. Mahayana Buddhism has, no doubt, received a fair degree of serious attention from Japanese theologians. But the overall impression is that they *neutralise the Buddhist challenge by filtering it through Western (often German) theological models.*

In Asia, it was Lynn de Silva who pushed the doctrinal confrontation to its ultimate limit. His investigation into the Buddhist theory of re-incarnation led him to revise his Protestant views on eschatology.[6] But the most daring achievement was his theological appropriation of the Theravada doctrine of *anatta*, namely, the non-existence of a human or any soul.[7] In the course of a much publicised dialogue between 'modernist Buddhists' and Christian theologians on the problem of God, the Buddhist's argument 'no soul, therefore no God' made an about-turn in de Silva's theological response: 'no soul, therefore God'[8] The Christian concept of *pneuma* was thus elucidated in terms of the Buddhist doctrine of *anatta*.

The Christian use of non-Christian doctrines is an apologetical method begun by the Greek Fathers, and is hardly fruitful in today's Asia as we have argued elsewhere.[9] Yet in this instance, de Silva has freed himself of the nineteenth century approach by not treating the *anatta* doctrine as a mere philosophical tenet (on a par with, say, that of David Hume who is quoted approvingly in the writings of 'modernist' Buddhists). Rather, de Silva saw in it the Buddhist equivalent of the principle and foundation of Christian spirituality: man's *creatureliness*. For de Silva always worked within the soteriological parameter of the two religions, though, perhaps, he did not give due recognition to the *gnostic idiom* of the Buddhists.

2. THE CHALLENGE OF THE GNOSTIC IDIOM

There are two irreducibly distinct languages of the Spirit, each incapable without the other of adequately mediating and expressing one's experience of God and of the world. *Gnosis* or the *language of liberative knowledge* is one; *Agape* or the *language of redemptive love* is the other.

In *Buddhism, karuna* or Love is an indispensable prelude to and an inevitable consequence of *prajña* or Wisdom which alone is considered intrinsically salvific. All affective currents of spirituality must at one point or other flow into the sapiential stream—not withstanding the pietistic schools of Mahayana Buddhism. The dialectics of Wisdom and Love, i.e., of gnostic detachment and agapeic involvement, constitutes a universally accepted dogma in the main-stream schools of Buddhism. Yet, when Buddhism speaks of Love, it normally does so in the language of gnosis.

Contemporary *Christianity* which is almost exclusively agapeic, has not only lost its earlier familiarity with the gnostic idiom, but has also inherited an anti-gnostic bias, though historians insist that there used to be an orthodox line of Christian gnosis and that the heretical gnoses were only the 'embroidery' along this legitimate line.[10] A glance at the socio-political history of Buddhist cultures should convince any Christian that gnosticism is not necessarily a-historical or a-political. It is the anti-gnostic bias that accounts for the Weberian sociologists' caricature of Buddhism as a 'world-*denying* asceticism' when in reality it is only a world-*relativising* affirmation of the Absolute.

Since language is not just a way of speaking about reality, but a way of seeing and experiencing it, the Buddhist challenge consists primarily in reminding the Christian that there exists *another* legitimate way of seeing and interpreting reality, as the following observations will illustrate. Theresa of Avila whose *God-experience* is expressed in the idiom of *agape*, refers to the mystical grace of 'suspension' (of senses and understanding) as being such an extra-ordinary and gratuitous gift of the divine Spirit that it would be presumptuous to make any human effort at acquiring it.[11] But whoever meditates under the guidance of a Theravadin Master is soon made to realize that this suspension' (*nirodha samapatti* or 'Cessation Trance' as the Buddhists call it) is a natural, predictable and humanly induceable psychic phenomenon not to be confused with Nirvāna which defies all human causality.

We are dealing here with *two language games*, each having its own set of rules. One game should not be judged/played according to the rules of the other. Thus while the Christian mystic speaks in terms of 'sin and grace', the gnostic vocabulary of the Buddhist Arahant knows only of 'ignorance and knowledge'. The gnostic process of realizing an 'Impersonal It' and the agapeic encounter with a 'Personal Thou' imply two modes of religious discourse, each having its own logic and its own grammar and syntax.

As with God-experience, so *also with regard to the external world*, we can adopt *two postures*: that of the Christian who delights in it and that of the Buddhist who keeps a critical distance from it. Each attitude has its own danger: stark consumerism and stoic indifferentism, respectively. Yet, today more than ever, we Christians should be made aware that gnosis and *agape* are the two eyes of the soul and that our partial one-eyed vision of the world has led us to the brink of a cosmic disaster.

Not inclined to revere or adore the Absolute because it is a non-personal reality to be realised through gnosis, the Buddhists tend, by contrast, *to attribute a quasi-personalist character to all that is not the Absolute*. Hence the cosmic forces are personified in the process of being relativised. In other words, the elements of Nature evoke a reverential attitude from humans. The cosmos makes *one ecological community* with man. Since Nature is man's cosmic extension, it cannot be mishandled without the whole human-cosmic continuum being disrupted. Buddhism knows a way of relativising the world *vis-a-vis* the Absolute without in any way 'instrumentalising' it.

Contrast this with *Christian Theism*. The Absolute is adored and loved as a Person while all else (human persons not excluded) shrinks to the level of an *instrument* to be *used* in the human quest for God. Ignatius of Loyola makes it the foundational principle of Christian asceticism.[12] The cosmic forces are thus regarded as impersonal things to be manipulated in the service of God and man rather than as quasi-personal beings to be treated with reverence or as silent companions in our pilgrimage towards the Absolute. It is this 'instrumental theory of creatures'—unchallenged by the gnostic vision of the world—that has paved way to the current impasse of technocracy with biospheric pollution growing into an imminent nuclear holocaust.

There was at least one Christian who was endowed with a two-eyed vision: Francis from Assisi. But he seems to have been a freak in Christendom!

3. THE CHALLENGE TO CHRISTOLOGY

The Indian sage seated in serene contemplation under the Tree of Knowledge, and the Hebrew Prophet hanging violently on the Tree of Love in a gesture of protest, are two contrasting images that clearly situate the Buddha (the Enlightened One) and the Christ (the Anointed One) in their respective paradigmatic contexts of gnosis and agape. In no other gnostic religion (Jainism, Daoism or Vedantic Hinduism) and in no other agapeic religion (Judaism or Islam) is *the person of the Founder* (if there exists one) accorded so central a place in his own kerygma as it certainly is the case with Buddhism and Christianity.

The parallel processes by which Gautama came to be revered as *the* Buddha and Jesus came to be proclaimed as *the* Christ indicate that any encounter between the Dhamma and the Gospel has to reckon with an eventual kerygmatic conflict between the two 'personality cults'.

The nineteenth century revival of Hinduism in India and of Buddhism in Sri Lanka bears testimony to this fact. The great Hindu reformers, despite their critical stance regarding Christianity, were willing to absorb the figure of 'god-man' Jesus into their soteriological scheme,[13] sometimes giving the impression that they were trying to rescue the founder of Christianity from Christian distortions! The Buddhist revivalists such as Anagarika Dharmapala, on the contrary, were known to have been not only critical of Christianity but also spiteful towards the very person of Jesus who, in their writings, contracts into a spiritual dwarf before the gigantic personality of the Buddha.[14]

Note, in this connection, that the Pauline missiology of the Letters to Ephesians and Colossians, which installed Jesus Christ as the one cosmic mediator and also as the metacosmic Lord over all visible and invisible forces of the universe, had already been anticipated in Asia by Buddhist missionaries who had enthroned the Buddha over all elements of nature and all gods, spirits and personified cosmic forces. This makes Buddhism the greatest challenge that the Christian kerygma has ever met in history—and *vice versa*.

Moreover, both the 'ontological' approach of traditional Christology and the 'soteriological and functional' approach of contemporary theologians find their vague analogies in the history of Buddhology.[15] Christians living in a Buddhist culture are therefore challenged to *revise* their *Christological formulae.* Perhaps, a new 'liberational' approach which would complement rather than cancel the past achievements should meet this Buddhist challenge. Since this suggestion has received sustained argumentation and careful formulation elsewhere,[16] I shall content myself here with merely making a few brief statements:-

(a) The only meeting point of the gnostic and the agapeic models of spirituality is the belief that *voluntary poverty* constitutes a salvific experience. Hence Jesus, as God's own kenosis and as the proof and sign of God's eternal enmity with Mammon, is an endorsement of the Buddhist ascesis of renunciation. THE STRUGGLE TO BE POOR is one of the two dimensions of Christian discipleship, and it coincides with the Buddha's path of *interior* liberation, namely, liberation from possessions as well as from greed for possessions.

(b) This same Jesus, according to the agapeic formula, is also the New Covenant, i.e. a defence pact between God and the Poor against the prevailing Order of Mammon. It is precisely when the poor struggle for their freedom and human dignity that God glorifies the Son as his Covenant before the Nations, thus breaking through the language barrier between gnosis and agape, turning *human love* into the supreme art of *knowing God* (1 John 4:7-8).

(c) Christ, at once human victim and divine judge of *forced poverty*, lives in the oppressed in whom he announces himself to be unmistakably available as the recipient of our ministry (Matt. 25:31-46). THE STRUGGLE FOR THE POOR is, therefore, the second constitutive dimension of Christian discipleship and is also the means by which Jesus is proclaimed the Lord of History. All Christological speculations that do not compete with Buddhological theories, flow from this liberational praxis.

(d) A Church that serves Christ who is in the Poor now (Matt. 25:31–46), without following Jesus who was poor then (Matt. 19:21), is a neo-colonialist threat to the Buddhists because it attributes to Christ a false political Messianism. Conversely, Christian communities that follow Jesus by their 'struggle to be poor', but do not serve Christ through a 'struggle for the poor', fail to proclaim Jesus of Nazareth as the Christ and the Lord of History.[17]

Notes

1. For a brief outline of these events and relevant bibliographical references, see A. Pieris 'Western Christianity and Eastern Religions' Part II, *Cistercian Studies* (1982) No. 2, 150-154.

2. See K. Malalgoda *Buddhism in Sinhalese Society* (Berkeley, 1976) p.192.

3. See G. Rothermundt *Buddhismus für die moderne Welt. Die Religionsphilosophie K.N. Jayatillekes* (Calwer Theologische Monographien, Band 4), (Stuttgart 1979) pp. 31-33, 115-116, 125 ff.

4. D. Snellgrove 'Traditional and Doctrinal Interpretation of Buddahood. An Outline for a Theology of Buddhahood' *The Bulletin of the Vatican Secretariate for Non-Christians* (Serial No., 13) 5/1 (March 1970) 3-24.

5. See *Buddhist Christian Studies* (University of Hawaii) 3 (1983) 3-60.

6. L.A. de Silva *Reincarnation in Buddhist and Christian Thought* (Colombo 1968) pp.161-163; 'Reflections on Life in the Midst of Death' *Dialogue* N.S. (Colombo) 10/1 (January-May 1985) 4-17.

7. L.A. de Silva *The Problem of the Self in Buddhism and Christianity* (Colombo 1975).

8. L.A. de Silva '*Anatta* and God' *Dialogue* N.S., 2/3 (September-December 1975) 106-115.

9. A. Pieris 'L'Asie non semitique face aux modèles occidentaux d'inculturation' *Lumière et Vie* 33 (Juillet-août-septembre 1984) No. 168, 50 ff.

10. L. Bouyer *La Spiritualité du Nouveau Testament et des Pères* (Histoire de la spiritualité chrètienne, I) (Paris, Ed. Aubier-Montaigne 1960) p. 34.

11. See David Knowles *What is Mysticism?* (London 1967) p. 86.

12. *The Spiritual Exercises*, No. 23

13. See M.M. Thomas *The Acknowledged Christ of Indian Renaissance* (Students Christian Movement Press) (London 1969).

14. See A. Guruge *Return to Righteousness: A Collection of Speeches, Essays and Letters of Anagarika Dharmapala* (Colombo 1965) *passim.*

15. I developed this theme in my *Teape Wescott Lectures* delivered at the University of Cambridge (England) in October 1982 (and soon to be published) under the title *The Buddhist World-view and the Christian Kerygma*.

16. *Ibid.*

17. See A. Pieris 'To be poor as Jesus was poor?' *The Way* (London) 24/3 (July 1984) 186-197.

(Note that, *Dhamma* or *Dharma* means the message of the Buddha).

Seri Phongphit

The Cooperation between Christians and Buddhists (Thailand as Model)

1. PAST CONFLICTS—GOOD LESSONS

WHEN TWO bishops of the Missions Etrangères de Paris stopped in Ayudhya, the former capital of the Kingdom of Siam (former name of Thailand), on their way to China in 1662, they found the Siamese so generous and religiously so tolerant that they were reluctant to proceed to China as planned. Then as the situation in China was reported to be unfavourable for evangelisation, the two French bishops decided to establish their mission in Ayudhya. One of their first tasks was to serve as go-between for King Louis XIV and *King Narai the Great* in their diplomatic relation. It was hoped all the time that the great king would one day be converted to Christianity, which would also mean the conversion of the whole kingdom. Their hope, however, never came true, although during his reign, King Narai was benevolent and supported the Christian Mission. Churches, schools and hospitals were contributed to by the King himself. This could be considered as compensation for the diplomatic service given by the missionaries.

The end of the reign of King Narai brought also the end of the royal favour and support. The successors of King Narai adopted another policy and were not favourable to the presence of the missionaries in the kingdom. Moreover, some of them found missionaries and lay Christians to be a threat to national security and Buddhism. In fact, at that time, *no Siamese citizen was allowed to become Christian.* Only members of minority groups and foreigners in the Kingdom could become Christians. This law was lifted only about 170 years ago, at the beginning of the Bangkok period.

It has always been said that Thailand has been very tolerant throughout her history. There have never been religious conflicts; there has been only cooperation. This is delusion and is unrealistic. One only needs to get closer to the historical facts recorded by both Thai and foreigners in order to realize how many conflicts have occured during three centuries of Christianity's presence in this country. The difference from other mission countries may be the number of *martyrs*. Only 7 Catholics were killed because of their faith during the persecution in the early forties. They are not yet proclaimed martyrs by the Church. Many Church authorities in Thailand are afraid that the cause would remind everybody of past conflicts and this would harm the present good relationship between the Church and the Thai people.

To talk about conflict here should not be to do the right thing in the wrong place. Cooperation between Christians and Buddhists in Thailand can be understood only in the context of the social and historical reality. Instead of being an obstacle to dialogue and cooperation, past conflicts have been good lessons for many. This is a reason why a brief analysis of past conflicts needs to be made before we turn to the actual situation today.

From the Christian side at least 3 points can be made.

(a) Since its arrival in Thailand, *Christianity* has always been *identified with Western civilisation*. 'Christian' was synonymous with 'Western' as 'Buddhist' was with 'Thai'. Very few from old Thai families became Christian whether before or after the promulgation of the law against conversion. The reason was that, once one had become Christian, one became a 'stranger' in one's own milieu. One was 'westernised' and had to leave the community to live in Christian 'camps'. There had been efforts by missionaries to apply Thai culture and way of life to Christianity, but these were too few and most of them were superficial. The missionaries did not understand Thai culture and Buddhism.

(b) The Christian belief that 'extra *Ecclesiam nulla salus*' caused missionaries and Christian faithful to look down on Buddhism and local beliefs. Expressions of this attitude became public offences which aroused many conflicts in the history of the Church in Thailand. 'Questiònes Disputatae' were written three times in the history of the Church in this country. Each of them led to serious conflict and caused difficulties for the missionaries and the Christian faithful.

(c) The Church has never been separated from *political power and interest*. The ups and downs of the Church often resulted from political situations. Persecutions during the Ayudhya period, during the reign of King Rama V in 1902 and during the Indochinese war between Thailand and France in 1940 resulted from the fact that the Christians were considered as followers of the

French and on the side of France. Christianity was seen as a means of French infiltration and subversion.

After *Vatican Council II* no one would expect that there would still be conflict. But it happened that in 1983 a group of Buddhists started to campaign against the Catholic Church accusing her of adopting a *new strategy to convert Buddhism to Christianity.* Catholics were accused of manipulating Buddhist doctrines, destroying the Buddhist religion and absorbing its good elements into Christian religion. There has been *no reaction* to this *on the part of the Church* in Thailand. Nobody admits any failture. The general feeling is that it is just a misunderstanding on the part of a small group of militant Buddhists. Again here no lesson is being learnt. Many Catholics still believe that it is justified to 'use' some of Buddhist doctrines to explain Christianity, no matter what the Buddhist themselves think. This is precisely what has happened many times in the history of the Church in Thailand.

2. INTERRELIGIOUS DIALOGUE—SOCIAL COOPERATION

These conflicts have taken place and are taking place in the context of traditional 'co-existence' and 'co-operation' between Christians and Buddhists in Thailand. There should be no need to mention the many areas of cooperation there are at present, since there are parallel situations all over the world, such as Church activities in education, health care and welfare.

(a) In Thailand as in many other countries in the world, a new mode of cooperation followed Vatican Council II. An Episcopal *Commission for dialogue* with Non-Christians was set up in order to promote mutual understanding and cooperation especially between Christians and Buddhists. Interreligious meetings and conferences are often organised. Buddhists, both monks and laity, are often invited to participate in important festivities and celebrations. There is more interest in the study of Buddhism, though this is more theoretical and textual than what is practised in everyday life of Buddhists. Some individuals choose to spend long periods in Buddhist monasteries or meditation centres in order to have 'direct religious experience'. Buddhist meditation is introduced into religious communities.

On the part of the Buddhists, there are also efforts made to dialogue with Christians. In 1969 *Buddhadasa Bhikkhu,* the leading figure in the Thai Buddhist world today, invited, by the Protestants, gave for the first time his standpoint on the question in his lecture on Christianity and Buddhism. That lecture had a great impact on both the Buddhist and the Christian milieu, since Buddhadasa is the inspirer of a Buddhist reform movement in Thailand. In 1979 Buddhadasa gave a series of lectures in his own monastery on 'Christian doctrines that Buddhists should know'. He gives his reflections and his own original interpretation of the Bible. Many of his opinions do not necessarily coincide with official Christian interpretation. However, they are an important contribution to interreligious dialogue, especially during this time of religious antagonism in Thailand.

(b) Christians and Buddhists in Thailand cooperate especially in *social works*. The fact is not isolated. Social cooperation is based on the openness of both sides. Buddhadasa's inspiration lies behind many initiatives both from Buddhist and Christian sectors. Hundreds of Buddhist monks have started to get involved in the social activities of their communities. This may be new for many of the new generation, although it was widely done in the past, but interrupted during the beginning period of the modernisation of the country at the turn of the century and continuing until after the second World War. Cooperation between Christians and Buddhists take place through the coordination of different Non-Governmental Organisations engaged in *human rights* and *development activities* in the urban and rural areas.

Since the late sixties the *Credit Union League* has been one of the most important forums for interreligious cooperation. In 1976 the Coordinating Group for Religion and Society, an interreligious human right group was founded by some leading Buddhists and Christians in order to denounce human right violations. Activities of the group during the first period focussed on political prisoners and political cases. In the last years many other issues have been also taken by the group.

In 1980 *Thai Interreligious Commission for Development* was founded again by leading Buddhists and Christians in the field of development. This is a forum, where religious leaders and lay people mostly from Buddhism and Christianity come together in order to share experiences in social action and in the life of the community. Many Buddhist monks have begun to programme a 'Buddhist "lenten" campaign' to arouse people to an awareness of social questions. Some Catholics who are engaged in development are starting to change their attitudes and ways of doing things. They realise that they lack knowledge of Thai Culture. They need to be more integrated into the cultural life of the country.

In many villages where Buddhists and Christians live together, there are development projects participated in by both Buddhists and Christians. The Catholic Commission on Development itself has its projects in many Buddhist villages. This is a kind of cooperation not backed by 'religious' interest. The Buddhists believe that this is not another form of proselitism.

Many of the monks join the forum to reflect on their experiences in order to find a 'contextual "theology"' for a programme now being carried out by both Catholics and Buddhists. This is a common effort drawn up on a common ground of understanding: *option for the poor, inductive way of thinking and developing religious principles* of actual and *contextual experiences.*

3. A PROCESS OF LIBERATION

It is somehow *paradoxical* that while on the one hand there is a group of militant Buddhists campaigning against the Catholic Church as an institution, on the other hand groups of Buddhists and Catholics are working together in the field of human rights and development searching for new religious perspectives. Dialogue leads to *unity and conflicts* at the same time. It tries to pass from the 'institution' to the Spirit, yet again it falls back to institution—becoming institutionalised. The process of inculturation gives way to misuse and manipulation. Prejudice still prevails. Fundementalism and triumphalism still exist deep down in the attitude of Christians.

The fact that cooperation between Buddhists and Christians in Thailand is effected *mostly in development activities* does not mean that it is possible to cooperate exclusively in this field. Development as understood by some Non-Governmental Organisations and by a group of monks active in cooperation is integral. It has both *spiritual and social dimension*. It is neither a matter of pure economic development nor of political awareness. It is a *process of liberation* from all kinds of oppressions: economic, political, social and cultural. The potentiality of the movement lies in the culture itself. The rediscovery of cultural and religious values returns self-confidence to the people. The renewal of religion and culture happens alongside of development activities. Many of the Buddhist monks engaged in social action practice meditation and have their own meditation centres. It seems that it is precisely these monks who are consistent and are the most significant support for the people's movement towards liberation. Cooperation with Christians somehow raises this movement to the international level, where similar experiences in other countries are learnt and applied to the local reality.

Interreligious cooperation still has a long way to go. Some questions and doubts are arising especially in the minds of official authority. If such questions should bring about conflicts within the Church, these are ideological. It is the way one views life, existence and faith in the context in which one lives. Only direct and integral interreligious experience will permit a Christian to realise what unity in plurality means.

PART IV

Chinese Religion and Christianity

Shu-hsien Liu

Christianity in the Reflection of Chinese Religion

1. ARE CHINESE PEOPLE IRRELIGIOUS!

CHRISTIANITY WAS probably first introduced to China from Rome in the *early Tang dynasty*. Emperor *Tai Tsung* issued an edict in 635 A.D. which showed a tolerant, even approving attitude toward the Nestorian sect. However, the sect became almost extinct after the religious persecution in 843 A.D. Buddhism revived, but not Nestorianism, more research needs to be done in order to find out about the causes of the historical fact.[1]

In the *late Ming dynasty* the great Jesuit pioneer, *Matteo Ricci* (1552-1610), became established at Peking in 1600 and developed an excellent relationship with some Chinese intellectuals. Western missionaries remained attached to the imperial court for almost two centuries until the early eighteenth century when they were forced by the so-called *Rites Controversy* to choose between the primacy of the pope and the Son of Heaven. There were not many converts for Christianity, the influence of the missionaries on the course of Chinese history was small, not to be compared with their influence on Europe through their reports on Cathay.[2]

Since the *late Ching dynasty* missionary activities were revived on a large scale, when China was not able to defend itself against the power of the gunboat from the West. After the two World Wars, however, Mainland China turned into a communist, atheist State. Hence we cannot but conclude that Christianity did not find much success in China. There must be reasons to explain the fact, and one of the important reasons may be the thought of the Chinese people.

75

One prevalent view is that the Chinese people are simply *irreligious.* *Bertrand Russell* had put it in the following way: 'China is practically destitute of religion, not only in the upper classes, but throughout the population. There is a very definite ethical code, but it is not fierce or persecuting, and does not contain the notion "sin". Except quite recently, through European influence, there has been no science and no industrialisation.'[3] Professor *Liang Sou-ming* (1893-) concurs with this opinion as he says in a recent article that 'the Chinese are the only people in the world who show little interest in religion, do not have much to do with religion, and may be said to be "an irreligious people"'.[4] Surprisingly enough even many Christian missionaries share the same view with the atheistic Russell. In 1964 when I attended an orientation programme at Indiana University, an elderly gentleman, who was formerly a missionary in China, voiced his opinion to me in the following fashion: China was a great nation, it had very high moral standards, only it lacked religious faith, hence Christianity would be a most valuable addition to the Chinese culture.

Unfortunately, however, the union between the two never happened. And we wonder why this should be the case. If *Paul Tillich* is right that only faith would contradict faith, then there should be no contradiction between the Chinese culture and Christianity. The fact that the projected union between the two never materialised makes one suspect that there is a deeper reason which prevents the union from actually happening. Is it possible that the Chinese do have their own faith which puts up a strong resistance against the Christian faith?

Should we continue to accept the traditional definition of *religion as faith in a supernatural God, then the Chinese are indeed an irreligious people. But* the definition is totally inadequate, as it cannot even cover Buddhism which no one would deny is one of the great religious traditions in the world, and it would be a contradiction in terms to pronounce that Buddhism is an 'atheistic religion'. Paul Tillich makes an interesting suggestion to redefine 'religion' as a state of *'being grasped by an ultimate concern'.*[5] On this view everyone of us cannot but have an ultimate concern whether it is money, nation, or the Christian God, even an atheist has his ultimate concern as he does have an ultimate commitment. Hence the crucial issue becomes that one must concern himself with a true ultimate worthwhile to be concerned ultimately. Perhaps Tillich went a bit too far as to render meaningless the ordinary use of the term 'religion'. But we may qualify Tillich by defining religion to be the ultimate concern *of a transcendent principle,* be it God, Brahman, or otherwise. Now the problem appears under a new light.

The Buddhist *Shunya,* the Taoist Way, the Confucian *Jen* (Humanity) appear to be competing ultimate concerns against the Christian faith. Under such an interpretation, *there is indeed religious import of Confucian philosophy*.[6] This new understanding of religion seems to provide a much better framework for us to discuss problems between Buddhism, Taoism, or Confucianism on the one hand and Christianity on the other. Even those who declare the Chinese to be irreligious are setting the Chinese traditions against the Christian tradition, and regard them to be competing ultimate concerns against one another. For instance, Professor Liang Sou-ming made the following statement in the same article where he said that the Chinese are an irreligious people: 'The intellectuals seem to love to give expression to the view that "the three traditions [Confucianism, Buddhism, and Taoism] are originated from the same source" and that "the five traditions (Confucianism, Buddhism, Taoism, Christianity, and Islamism) are actually united"[7]. Such a statement provides evidence that Professor Liang understands the Chinese traditions to be on the same level with Christianity as competing ultimate concerns. If he gets to know the new definition of religion, I doubt very much that he would still make the declaration that the Chinese are an irreligious people. It is rather that the Chinese are concerned ultimately with certain transcendent principles very much different from the Christian God.

2. CONFUCIANISM AND CHRISTIANITY: CLASSICAL DIFFERENCES

In this article I shall not touch upon the folk religions in China, rather, I shall concentrate on the so-called great traditions, especially *Confucianism,* which have exerted profound influence on the so-called small traditions. The search for Sung-Ming Neo-Confucian philosophers was without any doubt the search for an ultimate concern. *Ch'eng I* (1033-1107) had said of his brother Ch'eng Hao (1032-1085); 'From the time when, at fifteen or sixteen, he heard Chou Tun-i discourse on the Way, he got tired of preparing for civil service examinations and arduously made up his mind to seek the Way. Not knowing the essential steps, he drifted among the various schools of thought and went in and out of the Taoist and Buddhist schools for almost ten years. Finally he returned to the Six Classics and only then did he find the Way'[8]. Once Ch'eng Hao realised that 'our Way is self-sufficient', he no longer needed to drift among the various schools of thought such as Taoism and Buddhism.

The same may be said of Christianity. The three important questions for Christian theologians are *God, man, and the world.* We find that the Chinese philosophers are worried about very similar problems, only their thought has been formulated along a very different direction. For example, they have long since given up their faith in a supreme personal God, instead they have tried hard *to search for the Way*, whether it is Buddhist, Taoist, or Confucian. And they have also developed very different concepts of man and the world. Precisely because the problems are similar, while the proposed answers are divergent, we are in a very good position to conduct meaningful comparative studies of the two traditions: Chinese and Christian. In the following we shall examine the problems of God or the Way, man, and the world in that order.

(a) God as the Way?

The main stream of *Christian thought* may be characterised as a *supernatural monotheism*. Early Christian theology was under the strong influence of *Neo-Platonism* which taught a theory of emanation, the implication is that God is both transcendent and immanent. But when *orthodox Scholastic* thought shaped up, pantheistic mysticism was quickly denounced as heresy, as God was understood to have created the world out of nothing: there is a sharp distinction between the Creator and the created, and the world should not in any case be taken as part of God. Although Saint *Thomas Aquinas* allowed certain autonomy for reason, natural theology was still regarded as inferior to revealed theology. Cosmological and teleological arguments, even assuming they are valid, can only establish that God is, but cannot tell us anything about what God is; thus revelation and faith are considered to be superior to reason. In fact not only many including *Kant* questioned the validity of these arguments, but they are absolutely futile if the objective is to prove the existence of the *Christian* God. Therefore some contemporary theologians such as *Karl Barth* would not have anything to do with natural theology, God for them is 'the Wholly Other', beyond the apprehension of reason. Only God can relate himself to man, not the other way around. Man can only place his faith in Jesus the Christ. The transcendent character of God is most conspicuous under such a view.

On the contrary, the ultimate concern of the Chinese is the Way. *The Confucian Way* is both transcendent and immanent.[9] *The Doctrine of the Mean* has put it in the following fashion: 'The Way of the superior man functions everywhere and yet is hidden. Men and women of simple intelligence can share its knowledge; and yet in its utmost reaches, there is something which even the sage does not know. Men and women of simple intelligence can put it into practice; and yet in its utmost reaches there is something which even the sage is not able to put into practice. Great as heaven and earth are, men still find something in them with which to be dissatisfied. Thus with [the Way of] the superior man, if one speaks of its greatness, nothing in the world can contain it, and if one speaks of its smallness, nothing in the world can split it. The *Book of Odes* says, "The hawk flies up to heaven; the fishes leap in the deep." This means that [the Way] is clearly seen above and below. The Way of the superior man has its simple beginnings in the relation between man and woman, but in its utmost reaches, it is clearly seen in heaven and earth.[10] *The Way* is all-encompassing and mysterious, hence it is *transcendent,* and yet it is partially realised in the lives of men and women of simple intelligence, hence it is also *immanent.* The ultimate commitment to the Way and the faith in a supreme personal God show very different characteristics and are in some ways incompatible to each other.

(b) Original sin or anxiety?

Next, let us turn to the problem of man. According to the *Christian tradition,* man is made after the image of God, therefore there are certain noble qualities in man. But the Christian believers accept the myth of 'paradise lost': after Adam and Eve were banished from the paradise, the human descendents inherit the '*original sin*'. Although they are unworthy of being saved, yet God still sent his Son as the saviour to the world. Jesus was nailed on the Cross, and found another life beyond the life in this world. Those who place their faith in Jesus the Christ have got the chance to be saved, but those who turn their backs to Christ will be committed to the underworld and suffer unspeakable miseries after the Judgment Day. Protestants such as the Calvinists believe that we cannot save ourselves by our own effort, everything has to be dependent on the grace of God. Christianity has also to be regarded as a historical religion. Before the advent of Christ, people were expecting the coming of Messiah, after the arrival of Christ, people are waiting for the Last Judgment. Thus history has a meaning and a purpose. The biggest crime of man lies in that he has too much love and confidence in himself; only when he realises the depraved state of his being and repents, would he be given a chance to find a life of new being through his faith in Christ and God.

On the contrary, the very first statement in the *Doctrine of the Mean* says: 'What Heaven (*Tien*) imparts to man is called human nature. To follow our nature is called the Way (Tao). Cultivating the Way is called education.[11] What is implied here is that *human nature is essentially good.* As the *Doctrine of the Mean* says: 'Only those who are absolutely sincere can fully develop their nature. If they can fully develop their nature, they can then fully develop the nature of others. If they can fully develop the nature of others, they can then fully develop the nature of things. If they can fully develop the nature of things, they can then assist in the transforming and nourishing process of

Heaven and Earth. If they can assist in the transforming and nourishing process of Heaven and Earth, they can thus form a trinity with Heaven and Earth.'[12]

This may be said to be the Chinese doctrine of trinity. But this does not mean that the Chinese have adopted a superficial optimistic view of life. Lacking the consciousness of *'sin'*, the Confucian philosophers have developed *a heightened consciousness of 'anxiety'* in its place.[13] When Chu Hsi (1130-1200), the great Sung Neo-Confucian philosopher, tried to establish the orthodox line of transmission of the Way, he cited a statement from the *Book of History*: 'The human mind is precarious, and the moral mind is subtle, have absolute refinement and singleness of mind, hold fast to the Mean.'[14] Although the document is proved to be taken out of an apocryphal source, it does reveal the primary concern of the Confucian philosophers throughout the ages. No wonder *Mencius* (371-189 B.C.?) said that 'the way of learning is none other than finding the lost mind'.[15] And Mencius reported that Confucius said of the human mind: 'Hold it fast and you preserve it. Let it go and you lose it. It comes in and goes out at no definite time and without anyone's knowing its direction.'[16] The Confucian tradition believes that man has great endowment, and the great task of education is the discipline of the mind. This is the tradition of salvation through self-power, it is in sharp contrast with the Christian tradition which believes only in salvation through other-power.

(c) Negative or affirmative attitude towards the world?

Finally let us discuss the problem of the world. From the *Christian viewpoint*, the world and the creatures in it are created for the glorification of God. Hence it would be wrong for human beings to indulge totally in wordly affairs and cut off completely from the transcendent source. Jesus said that his kingdom was not of this world. *Augustine* contrasted the City of God with Rome. Christianity draws a clear line between the supernatural and the natural world. Even though the Church has developed into a powerful organisation in the world, and after the Renaissance there has been an ever growing tendency toward secularisation, the Christian message remains that of the other world, and the rituals are designed for the purpose. For instance, every week there is the Sabbath day, so that people may be released from their wordly cares and keep their mind on religious concerns. *Nietzsche* made a fierce attack on Christianity; as he saw it, Christianity had failed to say yea to the world, and he would like to spread what he called 'the message of the earth' in its place.

In the *Chinese tradition,* not only Confucianism has held an affirmative attitude toward the world, even Taoism and Chinese Buddhism have shown a high regard for nature and life in this world. Confucian philosophers believe that the world order is the result of an evolutionary process, and man has received the highest endowment among all the creatures on earth from Heaven. Therefore the only way for man to serve Heaven is to develop to the fullest extent his natural endowment. The leading principle for a Confucian philosopher is the *unity of Heaven and man.* As *Wang Yang-ming* put it: 'The great man regards Heaven and Earth and the myriad things as one body.'[17] For a Taoist philosopher, all the moral virtues and govermental organisations are artificial human devices that spoil the natural process of the Way, but Nature in itself is an inexhaustible source of creativity. The most amazing thing is that even Buddhism has acquired a completely new character after it has been imported into China from India. The starting point of Buddhism is to transcend the suffering caused by the cycle of life and death, while the wisdom of the Zen Buddhist is to accept what is here and now, and find joy in this life. From these instances we can see clearly the Chinese attitude toward the world.

3. POSSIBILITIES OF A BETTER UNDERSTANDING:

To sum up, for a person with a deep root in Chinese culture, it is very difficult for him or her to accept the Christian message. He or she would find that the Christian God is too transcendent, mystical revelation is too obscure to be be appreciated, there is too little faith in humankind, and there is not enough recognition of the intrinsic value of life in this world. I do not deny that there may be few truly devout Christian believers in China, but these exceptions would only prove the rule, as the majority of Chinese people are untouched by the message spread to them through the Christian missionaries.

Ironically, however, today the three great traditions in China such as *Confucianism, Taoism and Buddhism* are facing the same problem as Christianity since they are under similar threat from a modern scientific, industrialised civilisation. Hence all the great spiritual traditions in the world must joint forces to revive the meaning of the transcendent in a world which cannot care less about the so-called spiritual values. Christianity would find that it has a great deal to learn from the Chinese traditions which transmit a *balanced message between the transcendent and the immanent.* And the recent development within the Christian tradition has made it much easier to find rapprochement between itself and the Chinese traditions. For example,

Rudolf Bultmann has made a great effort to demythologise the Christian tradition; *Dietrich Bonhoeffer* has spread his humanistic message; and process theologians have put a great deal of emphasis on this world. I do not, of course, mean these new theological attempts are beyond controversies. But new ways of thinking are being explored, and some of the modern attempts will be moe than just fads, and would have everlasting influence on the future. In the meantime the Chinese also have a great deal to learn from Christianity. For example, the message of the *transcendent* tends to lose its edge in the Chinese tradition; too much confidence in human nature may lead to the undesirable consequence that there is not enough understanding of the dark side of human nature; and the ready acceptance of the world may prevent the Chinese from exploring the world from either the supernatural or the natural perspectives.

In sum, it is impossible for us to turn the clock back. Today's world is a pluralistic world, and it may be better to keep it that way, if we do not want to see it being devoured by a totalitarian authority. Different traditions may be allowed to keep their own faiths, they may learn from one another, and each may shine in its own way. And hopefully these new explorations may finally help to lead us out of the present age of crisis due to lack of spiritual concerns.

Notes:

1. See C. P. Fitzgerald *China: A Short Cultural History* (London 1961) p. 336.
2. See E.O. Reischauer and John K. Fairbank *East Asia: The Great Tradition* (Boston 1958) pp. 370-371.
3. Bertrand Russell *The Problem of China* (New York 1922) p. 202.
4. Liang Sou-ming 'How to Evaluate Confucius Today?' *Pai Sing Semi-Monthly* 96 (1985) 18.
5. Paul Tillich *Dynamics of Faith* (New York 1957) p. 1.
6. Shu-hsien Liu 'The Religious Import of Confucian Philosophy: Its Traditional Outlook and Contemporary Significance' *Philosophy East and West* 21 No. 2 (1971) 157-175. See also Julia Ching *Confucianism and Christianity: A Comparative Study* (Tokyo 1977).
7. Liang, the article cited in note 4, 21.
8. Wing-tsit Chan trans. and comp. *A Source Book in Chinese Philosophy* (Princeton 1963) p. 519.
9. Shu-hsien Liu 'The Confucian Approach to the Problem of Transcendence and Immanence' *Philosophy East and West* 22 No. 4 (1972) 417-425.
10. Chan, the work cited in note 8, p. 100.
11. *Ibid.* p. 98, with slight modification.
12. *Ibid.* pp. 107-108.

13. Hsu Fu-kuan *Chung-kuo jen-hsing-lun shih* (A History of Chinese Theories on Human Nature) (Taipei 1963) pp. 20-22.

14. 'Counsels of Great Yü' *Book of History* in the ancient script.

15. Chan, the work cited in note 10, p.58.

16. *Ibid,* p. 57.

17. *Ibid.* p. 659.

Julia Ching

The Challenge of Chinese Religion (Taoism)

1. WHAT IS TAOISM?

'WHAT IS Taoism?' asked Herrlee G. Creel in the book which bears this as a title.[1] He explains that it is foolish to try to propound a single, sovereign definition of what Taoism is, asserting that the more one studies Taoism, the clearer it becomes that the term denotes not one school, but a whole congeries of doctrines. The problem is all the more complex as the word *Tao* ('the Way') is used by every school of Chinese thought or religion, and because the English word *Taoism* is used to refer to both the so-called Taoist philosophy *(Tao-chia)* and Taoist religion *Tao-chiao)*. Besides, there has always been a certain shroud of secrecy surrounding Taoism, which, as a philosophy of recluses and for recluses, prefers anonymity and chooses to articulate its teachings in riddles, and, as an esoteric religion, discloses many of its secrets only to the initiated. For our purposes, however, it is important to say at the outset that while we are speaking of the challenge of *Chinese Religion* (Taoism), I do not mean by the word 'Taoism' the whole of Chinese religion. I prefer to think that *Chinese religion has many manifestations*, and that *Taoism represents, not so much 'one' of them, but those manifestations that are found on the folk level.* Even then, I must further qualify my statements by saying that this is not to mean that Taoism *is* Chinese folk religion, but that it may be said to represent the most influential strand unifying many diverse manifestations of folk religion, without being everything that folk religion stands for. According to this understanding, Taoism is the religious tradition which came down from very early times, indeed, from the times of oracle bones and divination, in a society where the shamans *(wu)* were venerated for their ability to communicate with the spiritual world—the world of the Lord-on-high, and of the other gods, including the ancestral spirits—and to heal the sick. In this sense, it is *different from philosophical Taoism,* that of *Lao-tzu* and *Chuang-tzu* through which the ancient religion was partially eclipsed by philosophical rationalisation. Although the Taoist religion that reappeared afterwards would revere Lao-tzu (both the man and the text), it would radically reinterpret his teachings as well as those of *Chuang-tzu. It* became *especially identified with the quest for immortality,* including physical immortality, through the search for elixirs in alchemy and yoga. It developed certain sects, including that which for many centuries had a hereditary 'papacy' with its base in the Dragon-Tiger Mountain of Kiangsi. (At present, this line of succession is facing the threat of extinction, since the last legitimate Taoist 'pope' died childless in Taiwan, and a power struggle between his widow and his nephew has, to date, not been resolved (January, 1985).)

2. TAOISM TODAY

Taoism, both yesterday and today, need not be exclusively identified with the immortality cult, since the Taoist religion *also encouraged practices of public prayer and penance, as well as of meditation and mysticism,* aimed at the union between human beings and the divine, which need not always have, as goal, the cultivation of this immortality. According to my interpretation, the Taoist religion is not the whole of folk religion, which includes also many Buddhist beliefs and practices, some of which (but not all) had been incorporated into the Taoist system. Neither should the Taoist religion be identified with the ancestral cult, which can also be traced to the earliest times, but which, while being an ancient tradition, has more bonds with Confucianism than with Taoism. Nevertheless the tradition of venerating ancestors has also penetrated Taoist beliefs and practices.

By the term 'Taoist religion' however, I do include the belief in *a hierarchy of gods,* (including mythical figures, as well as many who were divinised human beings) under the supremacy of the highest, often called the Jade Emperor, or, in Taiwan, *T'ien-kung* (colloquial for Lord of Heaven). I also include the belief in a hereafter, whether Heaven(s) or Hell(s), the complex ritual systems (including a quasi-sacramental regard for rituals of initiation, of purification and renewal in the life-cycle and development of the human person), the informative counsels regarding health and healing, and the admonitions to a moral life as the best preparation for a blissful eternity. In saying all this, I also recognise the real difficulty of separating Taoist beliefs and practices from Confucian and Buddhist influences. Perhaps, it is best to say that the '*Taoist religion*' I refer to is *a pragmatic designation*, useful for the purposes of discussion, since in actuality it is almost impossible to separate Taoist religion from folk Confucianism (in its moral teachings) and folk Buddhism (in its religious beliefs and in some of its rituals.)

I have talked about the ancient Chinese religion, and I have talked about the Taoist religion, in the present tense. This is because the *Taoist religion is still alive* and vibrant today, in those regions where the Chinese live (Taiwan, Hongkong, Singapore), and hs reemerged even in mainland China during the recent liberalisation. Besides, it resembles in many ways the folk religion found in Korea, which is dominated by shamanistic beliefs and practices, as well as in Japan.

3. TAOISM AND CHRISTIANITY: THE ENCOUNTER

Today, the encounter between Taoism and Christianity takes place especially in places like Taiwan, Hongkong and Singapore. We shall single out *Taiwan* for particular attention, and because it has the largest Chinese population outside mainland China. Taiwan has known of Christian evangelisation (both Protestant and Catholic) for over a hundred years. This evangelisation has met with a real measure of success—among two groups of people: the *aborigines* who live in the more mountainous areas or in the foothills (and are especially concentrated on the East coast, growing yam and peanuts, and whatever other crops their rough terrain would yield), nearly all of whom have become converts to Christianity, and the '*mainlanders*' (that is, those *families* which migrated to Taiwan over thirty years ago on account of the Communist revolution, and usually choosing to live in the cities), a large proportion (though not all of whom) have also become Christians.

Very few converts, however, have come from the *majority* group, the so-called *Taiwanese,* who, in turn, are divided into two dialect groups, the *Hokkien* and the *Hakka.* These are people of ethnic Chinese origin, whose ancestors came to Taiwan roughly three centuries ago, from the coastal provinces of Fukien and Kwangtung, to flee the Manchu invasion. They have lived under the Japanese occupation, and have kept, rather intact, their Chinese culture. They have also developed certain characteristics of a 'frontier people', tough and hardworking. Some of them have become Christians, especially Presbyterians. (The seminary in Tainan, in the South of the island, is a famous Presbyterian institution.) But most of them are resisting Christian evangelisation. And why?

4. THE CHALLENGE OF FOLK RELIGION FOR CHRISTIANITY

I believe that *the resistance of the Taiwanese to Christian evangelisation* can be *credited to the strength of the folk traditions, including the religious tradition.* The aborigines of Taiwan belong to diverse ethnic and linguistic groups, without *one* coherent tradition to which all can lay claim. Besides, their tribal religious beliefs had been tested by the changing times and found wanting. The mainlanders have fled to Taiwan, leaving behind their ancestral tablets and their age-old attachment to tradition. They too, experience a certain disillusionment with their former religions, and this spiritual vacuum made them more open to the proponents of Christianity. The *Taiwanese*, however, have preserved and developed a religious tradition to which they had tenaciously clung, even during several decades of Japanese occupation and the Japanese attempt to force state Shinto on them.[2] They frequent the tens of thousands of temples that dot the island of Taiwan, some of which have been constructed very recently, and by the very wealthy. Each of their homes resembles a small temple, with religious emblems, images, and a small altar with incense offerings to their favourite gods, and often also to their ancestors. Their spirit of tenacity, developed under persecutions, explains something about their continued attachment to their religion. But it is not an adequate explanation.

Taoism is a tradition which, in many ways, rivals Christian teachings, all the more because *it resembles 'folk' Christianity.* I am referring to the folk Taoist belief in a supreme being, governing over a spiritual universe of gods and goddesses, many of whom were historical persons, coming from all classes—including the popular Ma-tsu, the goddess of the South Sea, to whom the fishermen of South China in general, and Taiwan in particular, turn with such devotion. This pantheon offers certain resemblances to the Christian, especially Catholic, religious universe, peopled as it is by God, the Virgin Mary, and a multitude of saints.

For those who desire more theological sophistication, the Taoist religion offers its *doctrine of the cosmos and of cosmic process and harmony*, tracing all back to the *Great Ultimate (T'ai-chi)*, and the interactions of the two modes of *yin* and *yang.* But the T'ai-chi is not just an abstract principle, as it is in Taoist or Neo-Confucian philosophy. It is also identified with the Taoist supreme being, T'ien-kung. And indeed, the T'ai-chi *emblem*, in a circle with a curved line in the middle, separating a darker side from a brighter side, representing yin and yang, can be found in many, if not the majority of Taiwanese homes as well as the homes of some mainlanders. It is, indeed, the great East Asian symbol, which is also found on the South Korean national flag, and to it is attributed the power of protecting those who live under the emblem.

And the folk religion also offers its *cycle of festivals*, including those surrounding the lunar New Year, with its dragon dances and fire crackers, its prayers to the kitchen god, as well as the many *Pai-pai* rituals and festivals throughout the year, including those held in honour of the spirits of the deceased. Then there are also the *religious leaders*, the priests, who lead funeral rituals and perform other prayers, many of whom are also shamans or spirit-mediums, (there are also mediums who are not priests) and there are as well soothsayers, who can assist the faithful with their counsels and fortune-telling, explain the baleful influence of the stars,[3] and assist communication with the spirits of the beloved dead. There are even *certain texts* (the philosophical treatises like *Lao-tzu* and *Chuang-tzu* have been incorporated into the Taoist canon of scriptural texts, and given their own interpretations; the *Book of Changes*, a Confucian classic and a divination manual, is also part of this canon), including the Almanac, as well as prayer books and spirit-medium books. With such a religion, what else would one need?

In conclusion, it should be briefly mentioned that the *folk religion*, with all that it offers in its efforts to explain the universe and how it came about, the human being and his/her place in the universe, with a cycle of rituals to celebrate and placate the spirits, with a possibility for union between the human and the supra-human, even the divine, *lacks a philosophy and a theology in depth which could satisfy the modern human person* living in a rapidly changing scientific and technological universe. Besides, the Taoist fascination with what is usually considered as magic or the occult, may not attract the more rationalistic young. With the growing rate of higher education, it is beginning to lose its adherents among the more educated and urbane. This does not necessarily mean that a scientifically educated individual would automatically abandon his or her folk religious tradition. On the contrary, there are many, even among the greatest scientists, who are content with a few simple, religious answers to life in this world and perhaps even the beyond. Not only has science failed to answer many important questions of life, but science itself has its bonds with the occult, having been born, one might say, of alchemy and 'magic', and frequently offering possibilities that were once associated only with the magical.

In the rest of the world, the folk religion has survived, eithter in the 'bosom' of Christianity, as in Latin America, or is enjoying a certain renascence, as in the contemporary flirtation with the occult in some quarters of the West. Still, modern life, centered on industry, including high technology, makes such demands on all that one is no longer sure that the folk religion in Taiwan, which caters mainly to those living on and off the land, will continue to grow in the future, as in the past. After all, among those mainlanders who have opted for Christianity, many, for example, had once been devotees of folk religion, of Taoism. If these might change, why not others?

To whom, then, will the young and disillusioned turn—*to secular materialism or humanism, or to Christianity*? Probably to both. But at the same time, it looks as though the folk religion will continue to thrive for a long time, and that, with the present liberalisation of policy on China's mainland, the folk religion which was considered dead there, has once more reemerged. The *forms* of Taoism may be, to some extent, different, depending on the geographic regions, but its strength and tenacity is the same. And this is tribute enough to a tradition which has evolved during centuries, even millenia, to respond to and fulfil the human needs to relate not only to a natural environment, but also to the universe of spirits, combining a belief in a supreme deity with that in a multitude of intermediary spirits who may be more accessible to prayer, and who are interested in the temporary as well as eternal welfare of their devotees. For Taoism is a tradition which offers people the possibility of communicting with the gods, as well as that of *becoming* gods, either experientially in a brief trance, or in the hereafter. It affirms mystical experience, while encouraging a moral life. It gives consolation in distress, while offering the hope of the fulfilment of temporary needs and desires, including those of communal action, and political protest. With all its theoretical defects, it is a religion which has satisfactorily served countless generations, and may continue to serve countless more.

Notes

1. University of Chicago Press, 1970. See especially ch. 1.

2. Consult Alan F. Gates *Christianity and Animism in Taiwan* (San Francisco, Chinese Materials Center, 1979). I would have preferred 'folk religion' to 'animism'.

3. See especially Ching-lang Hou 'The Chinese Belief in Baleful Stars' in *Facets of Taoism: Essays in Chinese Religion* ed. Holmes Welch and Anna Seidel (Yale University Press 1979), pp193-228, as well as 'Taoist Monastic Life' by Yoshitoyo Yoshioka, pp 229-51.

Wang Hsien-Chih

The Coexistence Between Christians and the People on Taiwan

AMONG ALMOST twenty million people on Taiwan only 3 per cent is Christian. The rest of people more or less hold beliefs in folk religions, Buddhism, Taoism or Confucianism. The folk religions are popular people's beliefs which conist of certain native elements mixed with Buddhism, Taoism or Confucianism. There are more than 243 deities worshipped in the folk religions. In 1981 the number of temples and shrines was 5,539 while the number of churches was 2,169.[1] Besides these there are tens of thousands family altars of folk religions. Both the number of shrines, temples and churches is increasing year by year. In traditional Chinese mind the Church is acknowledged as a *'foreign' religion*. But Chinese people usually think: all religions are good for humanity and they teach people to do good. Therefore, Christianity can coexist with other religions in Taiwan although Christians are an absolute minority group.

Methodologically, it is very difficult to understand the religious phenomena in Taiwan without prejudice. To interpret a certain religion is a heavy task. How can we interpret religions with 243 deities? Many folk beliefs have no scriptures of their own, no historical records, no systematic organisations. Therefore, the writer attempts here to bypass the above problems by choosing the top seven deities, according to the numbers of temples and shrines they have, to analyse their basic characteristics. From the analysis they can be classified into four models of coexistence: 1. utilitarian model 2. moralising model 3. dominating model and 4. liberating model.

1. UTILITARIAN MODEL

The popular slogan that *all religions are good for humanity* actually implies that they are 'beneficial' and 'profitable' in terms of meeting the practical needs of people, e.g., psychological, physical, economic needs. The number one deity, *Wang Yeh* (王爺) who is worshiped in 753 temples, originally was a plague-god who healed people suffering from plague during migration from China to Taiwan in the seventeenth to the nineteenth centuries. But the function of Wang Yeh in recent decades gradually extends to the areas of fortune-giving, disaster-releasing, physical healing, etc. He almost becomes an 'almighty' and 'fortune-giving' god.[2] The top popularity and rapid increase of his temples signify the utilitarian character of folk religion.[3]

The number three deity, *MA TZU* (媽祖) who is worshiped in 510 temples, was acknowledged as a water-goddess. According to legends she protects people to sail across Taiwan strait. She is merciful and powerful. And gradually she is worshiped as an 'almighty' goddess who gives fortune to people when they are in needs.[4] The number five deity (397 temples) is *Hsuan T'ien Shang Tih* (玄天上帝) who has magic power to cast out almost all kinds of ghosts and evil spirits. He also heals people suffering from diseases. The number six deity, *T'u Tih Kong* (土地公) who is worshipped in 392 temples, is a popular land-god with a lovely face. He gives fertility to the earth, guards cemeteries and bestows treasures on people, especially on merchants. In every non-Christian tomb there must be an image of T'u Tih Kong. He is the most popular and welcomed deity in Taiwan. There is a popular saying: at the beginning and end of every rice field there is a T'u Tih Kong (田頭田尾土地公).

From an observation of the living phenomena of folk religions we can easily discern that such a strong utilitarian tendency in folk religions influences even the functions of deities in order to meet the *practical needs* of people. This folk religious utilitarianism also has a strong impact on social morale and other established religions. Taoism, Buddhism, Islam and Christianity are welcomed by people from this utilitarian perspective. And since people of folk religions have no concepts of scriptures and ethics, they can do whatever they like in order to achieve their pragmatic goals without any guilt-feeling.

2. MORALISING MODEL

There is a popular saying: all religions teach people to do good. *Confucianism* in its philosophical form is *basically moral-oriented*. The great teachers of Confucianism are deified by people, sometimes by emperors, in later days. Confucianism is the moralising religion *par excellence* in Taiwan. Because of its long history in China and Taiwan the Confucian moralising spirit has a decisive impact on other religions. *Ma Tzu* is a utilitarian goddess but she is also considered as a 'filial' goddess because according to a legend she was born a 'filial' girl. *Filiality* is acknowledged almost as the most important virtue in the Confucian moral system. The number two deity (578 temples), *Kuan Yin* (觀音), was originally a Buddhist god in India. But in Taiwan he is transformed into a goddess of *mercy*. She becomes a goddess of *good-will*. The number seven deity (356 temples), *Kuan Kong* (關公), was a national hero who was considered a just, faithful, wise, gentle and merciful person. He is deified to become a god of *justice* who protects people who have suffered from injustice. But this moral god is today, under the influence of folk utilitarianism, transformed into a god of benefit for merchants.

Christianity is usually linked by people with the Confucian moral teachings. The Christian teaching of Kingdom of God and Jesus's sermons on the Mount are often interpreted in terms of Confucian virtues even by Chinese or Taiwanese Christians. Moralisation and utilitarianisation of religious beliefs are working hand in hand so that even morality is sometimes utilitarianised. People of *Kuan Kong* worship like to print tens of thousands of the *Book of Virtues* (善書) in order to show their piety to god and to propagate moral teachings to people. But, as we know, printing books is not the same as realising the content of the book. Sometimes they print books and then forget the content.

3. DOMINATING MODEL

Long before the rise of Taoist and Confucian philosophy and religious cult China had developed a *political theology of the 'Son of Heaven'* and ancestor worship in the Shang and Chou dynasties. The king is deified, in this political theology, as the sole mediator between heaven and earth; the human empire is a reflection of the divine cosmic empire.[5] *The king as the Son of Heaven* is the only person qualified to worship Heaven, the high god of the divine cosmic empire, while the ordinary people should worship the spirits of their ancestors in order to pay filiality to their ancestors. And later on Confucianism has transformed the virtue of filiality to ancestors into a greater filiality to kings, i.e., the virtue of loyalty. Thus official political theology matched with the moral system of Confucianism constitutes a dominating civil religion to support the ruling class. Even today the ruling authorities in China and Taiwan celebrate Confucius' birthday anually and Confucius' temples are supported by official supply.

Some types of folk religions which emphasise moral teachings usually hold the same attitude toward this political theology. And conversely ruling authority encourages religions to accept such a political theology. Therefore, ruling class and religous authorities cooperate hand in hand to enslave people. In this sense religion becomes the 'opium of people'. The dominating civil religions sould like the Shintoism and Tenno system in Japan which enslave people and give rise to the so-called 'holy war' in Asia, military and economic wars.[6]

4. LIBERATING MODEL

Buddhism, I Guann Tao (貫真-) and Christianity have been viewed as religions with liberating motifs in China and Taiwan.[7] *Gotama Buddha* is worshipped as the number four deity (499 temples) in Buddhism as well as folk religions. He teaches about suffering of humanity caught in Karma and liberation from Karma through a profound self-insight into the nothingness of all beings to achieve Nirvāna. The number two deity, *Kuan Yin,* as a mother goddess of mercy also has the power to release people from the boundless ocean of suffering. The Buddhist view of liberation is mainly through a *self-enlightenment* and a *self-transcendence* over the chains of transmigration. I Guann Tao is also called *Five Religions in One* (五教合一) which consists of Taoism, Buddhism, Confucianism, Islam and Christianity. It worships the Taoist deity *Ungenerated Old Mother* (無生老母) as the highest one. It teaches about the Incarnations of *Tao* and *Mi Leh Buddha* (彌勒佛) as sage king or great master in history to save people from all kinds of sufferings, famine, disaster, plague, war, etc. The cosmic history is divided into *three periods:* Blue Sun Period (青陽期), Red Sun Period (紅陽期) and White Sun Period (白陽期).

Human history is now situated in the last period in which great masters incarnate are coming down from heavens to save 9.2 billion 'primordial souls' from the world who were predestinated and chosen by the Ungenerated Old Mother by means of secret teachings and rituals.[8] This other-worldly *eschatology* bears a slant of Gonstic dualistic religions and attracts a million people because of the suffering reality in Taiwan. It is still an 'illegal' secret religion in government's eyes but claims to have established more than three thousand temples (佛堂) since its propagation from China to Taiwan in 1946.

Christianity, besides being accepted as a religion of teaching good among many religions in Taiwan and China, is usually recognised as *the most liberating prophetic religion* because the leaders of two decisive revolutions in China in this century, i.e., Hung Hsiu-Ch'üan and Dr. Sun Yat-Sen, are Christians.[9] And recently because the Presbyterian Church in Taiwan has been involved in the human rights movement under the martial law and its general secretary Rev. C.M. Kao was sentenced for seven years in 1980, people on Taiwan became aware of the meaning of the Cross as a symbol of hope of liberation. Christian understanding and practice of holistic liberation which is non-self-centered and non-dualistic has been attracting people to get interested in and identified with Christianity eventually. But some conservative churches prefer the *status quo* to liberation. They become dominating, moralising or utilitarian Christianity just as Buddhism and Taoism have become so by identifying with the ruling authorities.

5. CONCLUDING REMARKS

People are always pragmatic-oriented. Consequently, the utilitarian model is the most attractive model of religions. But ruling authorities prefer moralising and dominating models in order to moralise people to support the *status quo*. Only *the prophetic minority* can uphold the liberating model to awaken the desperate mass in crisis. The four models coexist in Taiwan in a very subtle way. But because of the isolated and critical situation of Taiwan among international communities the crisis-feeling stimulates people to look for a liberating model of religions. Therefore, from the grass-root level *the liberating motifs* have become more and more conspicuous *in the practice of dialogue* among religions, although dialogue has been practiced on an intellectual level for many years without fruitful results. Religion should be 'lived out' rather than be 'discussed about'.

Christianity in the First World in the past century has been deviating from its liberating character and becoming utilitarian and dominating in many forms. From the challenge of the Third World the liberating model should be further pursued and practised in theology and mission today.

Notes

1. Yu Kuang-Hong 'Development of Taiwanese Folk Religion: Analysis of Government Compiled Data' in *Bulletin of the Institute of Ethnology,* Academia Sinica, No. 53, (Spring 1982) 67-103; *Seminar on Folk Faith and Society* (Taichung: Tunghai University and Taiwan Provincial Government 1982) p. 42.

2. Tung Fang-Yen *Taiwanese Folk Religious Faith* (Taipei: 1984, revised) p. 180 (Chinese only).

3. Li Yih-Yuan 'The Tendency of Development of Taiwanese Folk Faiths' in *Seminar on Folk Faiths and Society,* pp. 89-101, esp., p. 94 (Chinese only).

4. Tung, the work cited in note 2, p. 183.

5. Wang Hsien-Chih *The Concept of Cosmos in Tao-Teh-Ching and Its Theological Meaning* (Tainan: South East Asia Graduate School of Theology 1978) pp. 128ff. (Chinese only).

6. Shoji Tsutomu 'The Ideology of the Tenno System and Christian Responsibility' *Towards the Sovereignty of the People* ed., CTC-CCA (Singapore: CCA 1983) pp. 173-177.

7. Wang Hsien-Chih 'The Role of Confucianism, Taoism and Folk Religions in Shaping Some Perspectives of Chinese Political Vision' *Ibid.* pp. 146-152.

8. Wang Hsien-Chih, *Ibid.;* Tong Fong-Wan 'I Guann Tao: the Most Controversial Secret Religion' *Taiwan Journal of Theology* No. 2 (March 1980) 85-131, esp. 88-101.

9. See A.T. van Leeuwen *Christianity in World History* trans. H.H. Hoskins (New York 1964) pp. 365-381; C.S. Song *The Compassionate God* (New York 1982) pp. 192-215.

PART V

Towards a Theology of Religions

Paul Knitter

Catholic Theology of Religions at a Crossroads

TODAY ROMAN Catholic theology of religions stands at a perplexing and challenging crossroads. Using some of H.R. Niebuhr's categories from *Christ and Culture*, I shall try in the following reflections to identify stages in the evolution of Catholic theology of religions in order to show how this evolution has recently arrived at a new path never before envisioned or taken seriously. The pivotal question, naturally, is whether this crossroads leads to a renewal of Christian life and praxis or to an evolutionary deadend. To answer that question, I conclude with the suggestion that Catholic theologians of religions adopt the methodology of liberation theology. What is needed, I think, is a *liberation theology of religions.* Both this suggestion and the survey can be offered here only in a skeletal form that needs further development and criticism. The literature listed below indicates where some of that further substance might be found.

1. CHRIST AGAINST RELIGIONS

During most of its history, Christianity's attitude towards other religions has been adversarial. Although many of the early Fathers urged a positive view of non-Christians (e.g., through the *logos spermatikos*), *the dominant theological assessment of other traditions, from about the fifth to the sixteenth centuries*, can be summed up in a rather literal reading of Origen's and Cyprian's *'Outside the Church no salvation.'* Augustine's anti-Pelagian insistence on the gratuity of grace came to be equated, more and more, with its scarcity and confinement to the Church. (See the Fourth Lateran Council, 1215 and the Council of Florence, 1442).

With the Age of Discovery, thanks to the Council of Trent and such theologians as Bellarmine and Suarez, Catholic attitudes towards those outside the Church evolved from the earlier *exclusive* to an *inclusive* perspective—from 'Outside the Church' to 'Without the Church' no salvation. Saving grace was recognized beyond the visible boundaries of the church, but it could not operate without arousing in every person it touched an implicit, subconscious desire for membership in the Church. This view extended into our present century when theologians elaborated ingenious theories as to how someone could be a real though invisible or implicit or tendential member of the Church. Despite this view's more positive content, Christ still remained *against* the religions, very few theologians during these five centuries dared suggest that universally available grace might be mediated through other religions.

2. CHRIST WITHIN THE RELIGIONS

The *Second Vatican Council* dared make such a suggestion, and so it opened the way for an evolutionary leap in Catholic theology of religions. For the first time in the history of the Church, a magisterial statement recognised the value and validity not just of non-Christians but of non-Christian *religions*. What the 'Declaration of the Church to Non-Christian Religions' implied, *Karl Rahner* made explicit: other religious paths are, or can be, 'ways of salvation . . . positively included in God's plan of salvation'. Rahner, whose earlier writings stand behind the Council's Declaration, articulates the mainline version of Catholic theology of religions. His well known views rest on a threefold foundation—theological, anthropological, and christological.

Theologically, if Christians affirm God's universal salvific will, they must also affirm that God offers saving grace to every human being. *Anthropologically*, because of humanity's essentially social-historical nature, God's offer of grace, to a Christian as well as to a Hindu, must be *ecclesial*—embodied in some social-historical form. Certainly, Rahner concludes, we can expect the religions of the world to provide this ecclesial mediation of universal saving grace.

Christologically, however, Christians must say more about grace: it is always Christ's grace. As the 'final cause' or motivating goal for all of God's activity *ad extra*. Jesus Christ is both the *constitutive cause* as well as the *final fulfillment* of every human being's experience of grace. Therefore, all Hindus or Buddhists who experience grace through their religions are 'anonymous Christians'—touched by and oriented towards Christ and his church. Rahner proposed this theory of anonymous Christianity not for proclamation to outsiders but solely for Christian consumption—to convince Christians that God's saving presence is 'greater than humans and the church'.

As revolutionary as Rahner's view of Christ within the religions was, it turns out to be only a *partial* and *provisional* approval. Other traditions retain their validity *only* until Christianity and the Gospel arrive on the scene (which, Rahner reminds us, is not so easily accomplished). *Anonymous Christians* must be turned into explicit, fully ecclesial Christians. Only then is their innate quest for an 'absolute saviour' satisfied; only then do they have the security necessary for a full commitment; only then do they have the best possible chances for final salvation. In the end, therefore, the religions have no value in themselves; they are a *praeparatio evangelica*, a preparation for the gospel.— Rahner's theology of the religions, in its breadth of a new vision and in its traditional restrictions, embodies the mainline Roman Catholic view and is endorsed by theologians such as E. Schillebeeckx, P. Rossano, A. Dulles, R. McBrien (though they may not expressly use his theory of anonymous Christians).

3. CHRIST ABOVE THE RELIGIONS

Over the past decades, a number of theologians have opened a new stage in the evolution of Catholic theology of religions. They find that the 'Christ ithin' model, especially *the theory of anonymous Christianity, just does not fit their experience of other believers*. These theologians detect in other traditions no hidden presence of Christ nor an unconscious searching for an absolute saviour in Jesus. And to predefine Buddhists as Christians is not only offensive to them, it also blurs Christians' vision of what might be genuinely new and valuable in Buddhism. Finally, to define as Christian something that is only anonymously and invisibly present is a violation of the essentially visible, social quality of the Christian religion.

According to this new view Christ need not be within religions for them to be valid nor are they necessarily oriented toward or a preparation for Christian revelation. This view seeks to recognise other traditions as independent ways of salvation. Christ, therefore, is not a constitutive cause of saving grace, nor is the Church necessary for salvation. The primary purpose of the Church is not to *bring* but to *reveal* and *promote* the Kingdom of God that has been forming from the first moment of creation. And because *God* may *have more to say and do than what was said and done in Christ*, Christians enter *dialogue with* other religions not only to teach but to learn— to learn, possibly, what they had never heard before.

In seeking a more open and affirmative theology of religions, however, this new approach seems to assert more than it can theologically sustain. Most theologians who are dissatisfied with the way Rahner prejudges other traditions as provisional, dependent, or 'anonymously Christian' still affirm Jesus Christ as God's full, final, and therefore *normative revelation for all peoples*. In other words, if Christ is no longer the constitutive cause of grace and therefore no longer needs be *within* the religions to validate them, he still stands *above* them as the norm by which their validity is judged and in which they find their fulfillment. The religions may have an independent validity, but it is a deficient, unfulfilled validity.

Various reasons are given as to *why the normativity and finality of Christ must be upheld*. Kung argues that only with *Christ as* their '*critical catalyst*' can other religions adapt to our modern, technological world. Others hold that without some final norm, humanity will ultimately suffocate in historical relativism. For most of these theologians, however, the primary reason for insisting on the finality of Christ is to remain faithful to their tradition and to Christians' experience of Jesus as essential for the salvation of our human condition. *The finality and uniqueness of Christ*, in other words, is an *indispensable given of Christian belief*, that must be proclaimed to all at least as a 'friendly wager' (Hellwig).

This understanding of Christ as not against or within but as normatively *above* the religions has become, I think, a common opinion among Catholic theologians today; in different forms it is represented by H. Küng, H.R. Schlette, M. Hellwig, W. Bühlmann, A. Camps, P. Schoonenberg.

4. CHRIST TOGETHER WITH THE RELIGIONS

Here we stand at the crossroads mentioned earlier. A small but growing number of Catholic theologians are suggesting that a brand new approach to other religions is not only possible but necessary. Most of these theologians are well-worn veterans of dialogue. In their praxis of listening to the words of other believers and of trying to communicate God's word in Jesus Christ, they have found that the *given Catholic theologies of religions either do not really work or become, unwittingly, unethical.* When one of the partners in a dialogue insists, no matter how courteously, that s/he has the normative and final word, such a dialogue can finish only as one between the cat and the mouse (Maurier, Puthiadam). Both the 'Christ within' and the 'Christ above' models for dialogue with other religions are very much like the First World's model of *development* for promoting the economic welfare of the Third World; as liberation theologians have pointed out, such development subtly leads to further economic dependence and subordination rather than to true *liberation*. This is a form of neo-colonialism (Pieris, Ruether).

So these theologians are proposing a theological model that sees Christ *together with other religions and other religious figures*. Even more than the previous model, they urge the possibility/probability that, with Christ and Christianity, other traditions have their own independent validity and place in the sun. As the myth of the tower of Babel suggests, pluralism may be God's will. The *verum* (truth) may not be identical with the *unum* (one) (Panikkar). More concretely and uncomfortably, Buddhism or Hinduism may be as important for the history of salvation as is Christianity—, or other revealors and saviours may be as important as Jesus of Nazareth.—Yes, this is a crossroads.

I can only mention, not explicate, the *various theological frameworks* in which Christ is seen as *together with* rather than as against, within or above, the religions:

(a) Some theologians (Maurier, Puthiadam, Thompson, Knitter) suggest that all world religions constitute a *'unitive pluralism'* or a 'coincidence of opposites' in which each bears a 'complementary uniqueness'. Each religion (or religious figure) is unique and *decisive* for its followers; but it is also of *universal relevance* for other religions. Uniqueness, in other words, is neither exclusive ('against') or inclusive ('within' or 'above') but is essentially *related* to (with) other religions. There are, then, not simply many different paths to the top of the Mt. Fuji; the many paths must crisscross and learn from each other if all are to carry on their journey.

b) Theologians involved in the *dialogue with Judaism* (Ruether, Pawlikowski) take a more christological approach. Painfully aware of how traditional views of Christ have promoted a 'supersessionist', subordinating view of Judaism, they urge Christians to modify their notion of Christ as the *final* Messiah. Jesus is better understood not as final but as 'proleptic' or anticipatory—pointing to rather than finalising the Kingdom. Rather than 'normative', he is better understood as 'paradigmatic'. Norms tend to come in 'only's' and 'exclusives'; paradigms can be many and complementary.

(c) Another perspective (Panikkar) makes use of the *ancient Logos christology* and presses the distinction between the universal Christ (or Logos) and the historical Jesus. Certainly, Christians can and must proclaim that Jesus is the Christ; but they cannot simply state that Christ is Jesus. There is more to the Christ/Logos than the historical Jesus. The Christ can appear, differently but really, in other traditions and historical figures besides Jesus.

(d) One way of grounding and justifying this new view is to see it as the most recent stage of a *'natural' evolution* in Catholic theology of religions *from ecclesiocentrism* (Christ/Church against the religions) *to christocentrism* (Christ within or above) *and now to theocentrism.* No longer the Church (as necessary for salvation), nor Christ (as normative for salvation) but God as the divine Mystery is the centre of salvation history and the starting point for interreligious dialogue (Knitter).

Proponents of this new direction insist that they remain faithful to the essence of Christian tradition by continuing to affirm that *God* has *really spoken in Jesus and that* this message must be heard by all. But *really does not require only.* Christians therefore can be fully committed to Christ Jesus and at the same time fully open to God's possible message in other religions.—Or can they? Is Christian tradition being preserved or maimed in this new model? Perhaps insights from the theology of liberation can help answer these questions.

5.   A LIBERATION THEOLOGY OF RELIGIONS?

I would like to indicate how theologians of religions can make profitable use of the method of liberation theology, especially to explore and evaluate the new model of 'Christ together with the religions'. In making these suggestions I am urging a greater *dialogue between two of the most relevant, creative, and yet disparate, expressions of Catholic thought today*; there has been little conversation between *theologians of religions*, responding to the problem of religious pluralism, *and theologians of liberation*, responding to the greater problem of suffering and injustice. In recent years, however, it is becoming clear how urgently the two theologies need each other. *Liberation theologians* are realising that economic, political, and especially nuclear liberation is too big a job for any one nation, or culture, *or* religion. A crosscultural, interreligious sharing of liberative theory and praxis is needed. And *theologians of religions* are recognising that a dialogue among religions that does not promote the welfare of all humanity is not a religious dialogue.

Again, I can present only the 'bare bones' of what a liberation theology of religions might look like:

(a) Liberation theologians are guided by a *'hermeneutics of suspicion'*—the acute awareness of how doctrine is prone to become *ideology*, a means of promoting one's own interests at the expense of someone else's; such ideologised doctrine is always in need of revision. Adopting such a hermeneutics, a liberation theology of religions will affirm the need to revise traditional Catholic models and the way they have, perhaps unconsciously, subordinated and oppressed other religions.

(b) By beginning with liberation theology's *preferential option for the poor*, theologians of religions can clarify, perhaps correct, the theological *starting point*, as well as the *goal*, for their efforts to understand and dialogue with other traditions. The preferential option suggests that what makes it possible for different religions to speak to (dialogue) and understand (theology) each other is their common concern and different efforts to promote the 'salvation', or *liberation* of all persons, especially those most poor and suffering. This means that the foundation and main concern for any theological assessment of other religions is *not* their relatedness to the Church (ecclesiocentrism) or to Christ (christocentrism) or even to God (theocentrism), but how much they are promoting salvation—the welfare of humanity. (This approach implies that where religions do not share a concern for the welfare of humanity, dialogue is impossible, perhaps not worthwhile.)

The evolution in Catholic theology of religions, mentioned above, must therefore move beyond theocentrism to *soteriocentrism*. Such a move takes seriously the criticisms justifiably made of theocentric theologies—that in urging God as the common basis for dialogue, Christians are implicitly but still imperialistically imposing their notions of Deity on other religions which (like Buddhism) may not even wish to speak of God or Transcendence.

(c) Liberation theology insists that *praxis* is both the *origin* and the *confirmation* of theory or *doctrine*. All Christian beliefs and truth claims must grow out of and then be reconfirmed in the praxis or lived experience of these truths. Applied to a theology of religions, this means that Christians can claim that Jesus is God's final and normative Word for all religions *only* in and through the *praxis of dialogue* with other religions. Only in such an encounter can one experience and confirm the normativity of Christ. Yet such a praxis of interreligious dialogue has not yet taken place; indeed, it has only begun. A liberation theology of religions, therefore, will admit that at the moment it is *impossible* to make claims of finality and normativity for Christ or Christianity.

(d). The insistence of liberation theology on the *primacy of orthopraxis over orthodoxy* assures Christians that if claims about the finality of Christ/Christianity are not possible, neither are they *necessary*. The primary concern of a theology of religions should not be the 'right belief' about the uniqueness of Christ, but the 'right practice', with other religions, of furthering the Kingdom and its *soteria*. Besides,Christians do not *need* orthodox clarity that Jesus is the 'only' or the 'final' or the 'universal' norm in order to experience and fully commit themselves to the liberating truth of his message. Not those who proclaim 'only Lord, only Lord', but those who *do* the will of the Father will enter the Kingdom. (Matt. 7:21-23).

(e). This *orthopraxis of dialoguing with other religions* and of trying to promote with them humankind's *soteria* will provide a liberation theology of religions with the means to discern not only whether but *how much* other religions may be 'ways of salvation'. From their ethical, soteriological fruits we will know them. Through such an ethical hermeneutics, theologians might find reason to affirm Christ as a unique, normative liberator—as he who unifies and fulfills all efforts towards a full humanity. *Or*, they may discover that other religions and religious figures offer a means and vision of liberation equal to that of Jesus. Jesus would be unique together with other unique liberators—which would be a cause for Christian rejoicing. 'Anyone who is *not against* us is *with* us' (Mark 9:40).

According to a liberation theology of religions, whether such orthodox discernments about uniqueness and finality are made or not is, in the final analysis, perhaps not that important, as long as we, with all peoples and religions, are seeking first the Kingdom and its justice (Matt. 6:33).

Literature

Christ Within the Religions
A. Dulles *Models of Revelation* (New York 1983).
R. McBrien *Catholicism* (Minneapolis 1981) pp. 245-77.
K. Rahner, *Theological Investigations* Vol. 5 (New York 1964) pp. 115-34.
Id, Foundations of Christian Faith (New York 1978).
P. Rossano 'Christ's Lordship and Religious Pluralism in *Christ's Lordship and Religious Pluralism* eds. G. Anderson and T. Stransky, (Maryknoll 1981) pp. 96-110.
E. Schillebeeckx 'The Church and Mankind' *Concilium* 1 (1965) 69-100.

Christ Above the Religions
W. Bühimann *God's Chosen Peoples* (Maryknoll 1983).
A. Camps *Partners in Dialogue: Christianity and Other World Religions* (Maryknoll 1983).
M. Hellwig *Jesus the Compassion of God* (Wilmington 1983) pp. 127-55.
E. Hillman 'Evangelism in a Wider Ecumenism: Theological Grounds for Dialogue with Other Religions' *Journal of Ecumenical Studies* 12 (1975) 1-12.
H. Kung *On Being a Christian* (New York 1976) pp. 89-118.
Id. Christentum und Weltreligionen (Munich 1984).
H.R. Schlette *Towards a Theology of Religions* (London 1966).

P. Schoonenberg 'The Church and Non-Christian Religions' *The Evolving Church* ed.
D. Flanagan, (Staten Island 1966) pp. 89-109.

Christ Together With the Religions
P. Knitter *No Other Name? A Critical Survey of Christian Attitudes toward the World Religions* (Maryknoll 1985).
H. Maurier 'The Christian Theology of the Non-Christian Religions' *Lumen Vitae* 21 (1976) 59-74.
R. Panikkar *The Unknown Christ of Hinduism* (Maryknoll 1981 [rev.ed.]).
J. Pawlikowski *Christ in the Light of the Christian Jewish Dialogue* (New York 1982).
A. Pieris 'The Place of Non-Christian Religions and Cultures in the Evolution of Third World Theology' *Irruption of the Third World: Challenge to Theology* eds. V. Fabella and S. Torres, (Maryknoll 1983) pp. 113-39.
Id. 'Speaking of the Son of God in Non-Christian Cultures' *Concilium* 153 (3/1982) 65-70.
I. Puthiadam 'Christian Faith and the Life in a World of Religious Pluralism' *Concilium* 135 (5/1980) 99-112.
R. Ruether *To Change the World: Christology and Cultural Change* (New York 1981).
W. Thompson *The Jesus Debate* (New York 1986).

Leroy Rouner

Theology of Religions in Recent Protestant Theology

1. CONFRONTATION WITH WORLD RELIGIONS—A CHALLENGE FOR PROTESTANT THEOLOGY

THE CENTRAL question for recent Protestant theological reflection on religions is, '*How does religious pluralism affect the Christian understanding of God?*' The question comes from the belated recognition that our global city includes non-Christian religions of high moral stature and theological sophistication which challenge fundamental Christian conceptions of who God is, what God wants, and even whether religion needs a concept of God at all. *Protestant thought has always taken its cultural horizon seriously* because of its emphasis on the sovereignty of a God who works in history. Thus, for example, *Darwinism* could not be ignored by Protestant thought, as it was by the traditional religions. The present confrontation with the life and thought of other world religions is comparable to the earlier encounter with Darwinism. In that conflict nineteenth-century Protestant thought accepted science as a value, and not simply a fact of life. Today it accepts religious pluralism as a value, and not simply a fact of life. The motivation today is different, however. Nineteenth-century Protestant thought had already adopted scientific thinking as its own internal criterion for truth. When biological science challenged Christian views on the origins of human-kind the challenge was as much internal to Protestant thought as it was external. The response to Darwinism was necessary for the preservation of Protestantism's intellectual integrity.

In the *confrontation with world religions* the challenge is primarily moral and historical. This moral challenge has two driving forces, one relatively weak, and one relatively strong. The relatively weak driving force is the embarrassing realisation that claims for the superiority of Christianity over other world religions have been based, in part, on ignorance. Most Christians were neither well acquainted with the subtleties of Buddhist doctrine, for example, nor knowledgeable about the functional values and cultural intricacies of actual Buddhist life. With acquaintance comes respect and uncertainty about one's previous convictions. The relatively strong driving force, seen also in current theologies of liberation, is the conviction that *Christians have been responsible for colonising* and even subjugating people of the Third World. For most Protestant theology of religions political and economic repentance for the sins of Western colonialism now also includes theological repentance for the sins of Western Christianity in denigrating the religions of the Third World. Hence the sharpest *criticism of Protestant missions* in India, for example, comes not from Indian Hindus or Muslims but from Western Protestant theologians. In the mid-60s when the Hindu philosopher/statesman Sarvepalli Radhakrishnan was President of India, he regularly expressed his appreciation for missionary medical and educational work by exhorting his countrymen to embody 'the missionary spirit'. In the West, however, 'the missionary spirit' was much criticised for its theological triumphalism and social and political collusion with colonialism.

This strong driving force of moral repentance explains the otherwise inexplicable *asymmetry in current inter-religious dialogue*. Dialogue is often described as a symmetrical coming together of people from various religious communities to gain greater mutual understanding. This explanation assumes a common motivation for dialogue among the world's religions. In fact, however, interreligious dialogue is asymmetrical, largely initiated, funded, and *motivated by Western Christian groups*. The primary motivating purpose of dialogue is to salve the conscience of post-colonial Western Christians and solve the theological challenge of pluralism to the Western Christian understanding of God. The Western Christian invitation to dialogue pre-supposes a common ground which does not yet exist, since the moral and intellectual motivations for dialogue are Western and Christian in origin.

For example, the most active current interreligious dialogue is probably among *Christians and Buddhists*. Buddhists have neither the bad conscience of the postcolonial West, since they are Easterners, nor theological difficulties with the doctrine of God, since Buddhism has no doctrine of God. As a result interreligious dialogue is regularly at cross-purposes, and dialogue conference reports are usually marked by intellectual confusion and the repetition of familiar but unintegrated Western Christian themes undergirded by moral exhortation concerning the importance to world peace and human community of such 'coming together'. Interreligious dialogue conferences are socially and culturally useful but not yet theologically creative. More interesting is the struggle of individual Protestant thinkers to shape a theology of religions.

2. PROTESTANT THINKERS BETWEEN EXCLUSIVISM AND PLURALISM

The historical background to this struggle is summarised elsewhere[1]. Protestant thought had previously regarded Christianity as either the best religion (*Schleiermacher*) or the true faith beyond religion (*Barth*). In either case, it linked the authenticity and seriousness of faith to the exclusive claims of Christianity over against the non-Christian religions. To hold Christian faith seriously and authentically was to hold it exclusively. But today *exclusivism*, once a value, has become *a problem*; and *pluralism*, once a problem, has become *a value*. Our global human family includes various religious communities. It is now widely held that no one of them should claim to be the best or the only true one. Such claims smack of colonialism or ignorance. Most Protestant theology also rejects any posited notion of transcendent truth, and begins rather from an historical notion of experiential truth.

This move is enough to characterise contemporary Protestant theology of religions as neoliberal, since not even *Tillich* among the neo-orthodox theologians of the past generation accepted *'experience' as a valid source for our knowledge of God*. Tillich says that experience is not the source but the medium.[2] Most Protestant theology of religions today is saying that experience is the source. The distinction between transcendence and immanence thus becomes increasingly uncertain.

The effect which this move has had on the doctrine of God is considerable. Protestant neo-orthodox thought was predominantly trinitarian, focused on Christology. Much *Protestant theology today has virtually eliminated Christology as a distinctive source for our knowledge of God*. The turn has been toward a notion of God emphasizing 'what we all hold in common', best expressed in *John Hick's* genial view that 'God Has Many Names'. John Cobb and Jürgen Moltmann are major exceptions to this generalisation.

Cobb presents a neo-Whiteheadian Christology 'from below', based on process theology's conviction that knowledge comes through the on-going *process of historical experience*, and that the historical Christ is therefore a critical way of knowing who God is. *Moltmann* presents a neo-Barthian Christology 'from above', based on the biblical conviction that knowledge of

God comes through the ongoing *process of God's revelation* of his Word, which is encountered definitively in Jesus, the Christ. We will return to these two points of view in conclusion. First, however, we need to consider the positions of three thinkers whose views characterise and influence this growing conversation. They are Ninian Smart, John Hick, and Wilfred Cantwell Smith.

3. THE PLURALIST, BUT NOT RELATIVIST POSITION

Smart, Hick, and *Smith* all find *the notion of 'religion' unsatisfactory.* Barth's criticism of 'religion' sought to protect the transcendent distinctiveness of Christianity's God over against the world powers and humanly constructed idols of all social and cultural institutions, including religions. Smart, Hick, and Smith, on the other hand, are all sympathetic to *Gordon Kaufman's* neo-Kantian view that theology is always and only a constructive exercise of the human imagination.

Barth was no stranger to the Kantian limitation on pure reason but solved the epistemological dilemma with the *radical category of revelation.* For Barth we could know nothing definitive about the God who is really God had not God revealed himself in Jesus Christ. The revelation in Christ is therefore the single source of certain knowledge about the One God who is Lord over all the many gods of the world's theological imagination. Here, however, exclusivism becomes unavoidable since the definitive source of our knowledge of God is in Christ.

For Smart, Hick, and Smith the *revelation of God in Christ is not sui generis but continuous* with, and of the same order as, the knowledge of God expressed in other religious traditions. Barth criticised the notion of religion because it compromised the sovereignty of a Transcendent God. Smart, Hick, and Smith criticise it because it compromises the human bond they both see and seek among the world's various believers. They see it historically in certain common practices and beliefs. They seek it theologically in a *notion of the Transcendent* which will do justice to the various names for the divine which the human theological imagination project on ultimate reality.

This broadened analysis of religion is not uniform. *Smart* speaks of *'worldviews'* in order to include ideologies such as Marxism and do justice to the complex interaction between religious belief and other cultural commitments which are also strongly held. He therefore analyses religion in terms of its doctrine, myth, ethics, ritual, and experiential and social dimensions.[3]

Smith, in his monumental '*The Meaning and Ends of Religion*' (1963), argued that the concept of distinctive, self-sufficient religions is fairly recent and cannot bear scrutiny as a descriptive, *historical category*. In '*Towards a World Theology*' (1981) he argues for the unity of humankind's religious history and illustrates that argument with narratives and doctrines which exist in only slightly *different versions* in many of the great religious traditions. Smith speaks of personal 'faith' in given communities which are historically in process of change and development. He continues to speak of 'God', however, as the common transcendent reality eliciting faith.

Hick also emphasises the continuous change in religious life in opposing absolute claims by any tradition. He criticises Christian doctrines of Incarnation and Trinity as exclusivistic and suggests that these are not 'precise metaphysical truths' but rather '*imaginative constructions* giving expression—in the religious and philosophical language of the ancient world—to the Christian's devotion to Jesus as the one who has made the heavenly Father real to him'.[4]

For Hick the important process taking place in each of the great religious traditions is the transformation of human existence from self-centeredness to centeredness on Reality or the Eternal One.

Exclusivism is therefore overcome and pluralism celebrated by emphasising the *poetic or mythical character of all absolute religious claims*. A common theme is that we are each saved by the God who comes to us through the religious and cultural context of ideas and practices in our particular community. This essentially Hindu notion of religion is accompanied by a notion of history which is also essentially Hindu, the idea that all religious truth in this realm of *nama* and *rupa* ('names' and 'things') is necessarily proximate and mythic.

Even for *Tillich*, whose philosophy of symbol covered most theological language, one nonsymbolic theological statement was required in order to make the notion of symbol itself meaningful, since symbols are always *of* something. That statement was that *God is the Ground of Being*, or Being Itself. Since any absolute (literal) statement is rejected by Smart, Hick, and Smith, relativism seems inevitable.

Smart, however, argues for a '*soft nonrelativism*' in religious affirmations, since there is 'a religious ultimate lying beyond this world'.[5]

Smith also intends to avoid relativism. He believes that it *is always God who saves us*, whatever our tradition, and finds the God revealed to him in Jesus Christ to be the same as the God revealed in the Qur'an to al-Ghazzali. *Hick* proposes a Christology devoid of any absolute claims. He seems to presuppose that Reality or the Eternal One is absolute in itself, however, even though none of our statements about it can be absolute.

These Protestant protestations against relativism become dogmatism without some explanation of how we know God to be what we claim. For all the emphasis on common ground among historical religious communities, there has not yet been a systematic attempt to show which specific beliefs are, in fact, common, although the World Council of Churches has made efforts in this direction. Such an attempt would be a necessary element in the new natural theology of religions being proposed. An *alternative* would be a *common mystical theology of God*, but there is no hint of such a programme in the present literature. We are left with an empty concept of God. Since theology, like nature, abhors a vacuum, this emptiness tends to be filled with content from one's own tradition. The intention is *to honour the human community's religious diversity*. The danger, however, is that an empty concept of God, which is of no serious religious interest to anyone, will make an articulate cloak for the absolute claims of one's own tradition.

4. THE CHRISTOCENTRIC, BUT NOT EXCLUSIVIST POSITION

Wolfhart Pannenberg, John Cobb, and Jürgen Moltmann have all argued that *Christology* can be *nonrelativistic* without being exclusive. *Pannenberg*, like Smith and Hick, emphasises the significance of historical change and development for a theology of religions. Like Smith he also believes that the history of religions is now a single, universal history in which the various gods are in competition, thus changing all religions. He distinguishes, however, between the religions which have been able to acknowledge change and those who have not because they have been bound to their religious tradition. It was Jesus who first forsook tradition in religious life for the sake of the coming reign of God. *The One God is thus revealed in all religious history as the Transforming One.* The distinctive Christian claim is simply that the God we learn about through contact with other religions is this Transforming One who is the God revealed in Jesus.

John Cobb is critical of Smith and Hick in their argument that a transcendent God is the object of worship in all religions. Cobb counters that *the idea of God is different from the notion of Emptiness* in Mahāyāna Buddhism, for example, and that this difference needs to be recognised. He points out that a Christocentric theology puts special emphasis on historical process, so central to the thought of both Hick and Smith. Cobb emphasises faithfulness to *the living Christ of history* who leads us into new truth. Like Pannenberg, he emphasises God's revelation in Christ as *opening us to the future work of the saving God* within us and among us. Cobb affirms that the totality of Jesus is the Christ, the universal revealing and saving presence of God; but he acknowledges that the reality of the Christ is not limited to the historical Jesus. He is thus in a position to find Christ in other religious traditions as, for example, *Raimundo Panikkar* does in '*The Unknown Christ of Hindiusm*' and *M. M. Thomas* does in his more historically oriented '*The Acknowledged Christ of the Indian Renaissance.*'

Jürgen Moltmann argues that the Barthian strictures against religion were directed toward religion as the self-assertion of humankind, especially in Christianity. For him the essential element in Christian life is the conviction that *Christ* has come and was sacrificed for the *reconciliation of the whole world*. Thus set free from 'religion' of all sorts he can call for a dialogue with people of other faiths and ideological persuasions in which Christian people are open to being changed. The aim of the *Christian mission* is to infect people of all religions with the spirit of hope and love and responsibility for the world in which we all live together.

For Moltmann, however, this freedom to make a qualitative alteration in the way people feel and think and act is possible because of the *cross* of Christ. The more central the cross becomes to human life and thinking, the more open is our interest in others, including their religion. For Moltmann it is not necessary for one to acknowledge the Christ event in order to be included in it. He does not develop a view of the role the historical Christ plays within the life of a non-Christian religious community, as *M. M. Thomas* has done, although one can expect Cobb and Moltmann to be sympathetic to future research in this area.

CONCLUSION

How significant, then, is current Protestant theology of religions for the future of Christian theology? My view, already stated, is that this issue is as formative for Protestant thought today as the struggle with Darwinism was in an earlier generation. The imperative for religious dialogue will increasingly join with the imperatives of liberation theologies, on the side of freedom and against oppressions of all sorts. The critical question is whether the affirmations of freedom and openness toward other religions will have positive substance or be a negative reaction to past guilt on the part of postcolonial Western Christians.

Guilt is still too much a part of the motivation for Protestant theology of religions. A *guilty Christian conscience* is ostensibly concerned with the authentic life of others, but in fact is self-absorbed, seeking primarily to make amends for past wrongdoing. Christians must be faithful to our affirmation that Christ's sacrifice on the cross has freed us from guilty bondage to sin and death in order to be *open to the future*. Openness to the future means openness to the deepest questions which people are asking about the most critical issues in their lives. The world does not care whether or not Protestant theologians have recovered from their guilt over their exploitative *colonial past*, or even whether they can solve the theological problem presented by their pluralistic cultural horizon. It cares whether or not they have a saving word about the future. Dr. *Abid Hussain*, the Muslim president of the Islam and the Modern Age Society in India, put the serious dialogue question succinctly when he asked; 'What is the best your religion has to offer to the problems we all face?'

Our best is not the idea of an empty God. This notion is not Good News for anyone; it only combines the worst of both Western and Eastern worlds. John Cobb is right in saying that 'to sacrifice belief in the Incarnation for the sake of dialogue would not only impoverish us but would also take from us our most potential gift to the dialogue partner'[6]. As interreligious dialogue moves beyond its origins in Christain moral concern to salve its conscience for colonial oppression and intellectual concern to solve its theological problem of pluralism, it will look increasingly to those Christocentric theologies which have developed an open, vulnerable, yet faithful affirmation that God was indeed in Christ, reconciling the world to himself.

Notes:

1. See my Introduction to ed. L. Rouner, *Religious Pluralism* (Notre Dame, Ind. 1984) pp. 1-13, and in John Cobb 'The Meaning of Pluralism for Christian Self-Understanding' in the same volume (pp. 161-179), as well as in Cobb. *Beyond Dialogue* (Philadelphia, 1982), pp. 1-25.
2. P. Tillich *Systematic Theology* 3 vols. (Chicago 1951-63) I, p.42.
3. N. Smart *Worldviews* (New York 1983) pp. 1-11.
4. J. Hick *God Has Many Names* (Philadelphia 1980) p.125.
5. N. Smart 'Buddhism, Christianity, and the Critique of Ideology' in *Religious Pluralism* ed. L. Rouner (Notre Dame Ind. 1984), p.150.
6. J. Cobb *Beyond Dialogue* cited in note 1, at p. 45.

Synthesis

Hans Küng

Towards an Ecumenical Theology of Religions: Some Theses for Clarification

1. FOUR INADEQUATE OUTLINE POSITIONS

a. THE *ATHEIST position:* no religion is true. Or else: all religions are equally untrue. Nevertheless our pure, theoretical reason is bound to this world and cannot reach far enough definitively to reject the question whether religion in reality corresponds to nothing or to an Absolute. To give one's assent to some ultimate ground, source or sense of the world and human life such as is maintained in any of the great religions is not a matter of strict proof but of reasonable trust, which, however, reposes on good grounds.

b. The *absolutist position*: only one unique religion is true. Or else: all other religions are untrue. Nevertheless the dogma of the Fourth Lateran Council (1215) and of the Council of Florence (1442). *'EXTRA ECCLESIAM NULLA SALUS',* has no longer been held even by the Catholic Church since Vatican II, even though it is not often corrected. It is still being debated within the World Council of Churches, although it contradicts the will to universal salvation and the admittedly marginal but always perceptible utterances about the heathen in Scripture, so that even the later Karl Barth was obliged to accept 'other lights' besides the 'one light'.

c. The *relativistic position*: each religion is true. Or else: all religions are equally true. Nevertheless anybody who is really acquainted with the world religions can hardly maintain that they are all alike, especially when he or she thinks about the different basic types of mystical or prophetic religions. Even recourse to some supposedly overall similar religious (mystical) experience does not resolve the problem, because every religious experience is through and through an interpreted experience and so is penetrated by the relevant religious tradition and its various forms of expression.

d. The *inclusivist position*: one religion alone is the true one. Or else: all religions have a share in the truth of the one religion. Nevertheless, whether in the Indian variants (all religions represent only different levels of the one universal truth) or in the Christian variants (all religious people are anonymous Christians) the other religions are in fact relegated to a lower or a partial knowledge of the truth in such a way that one's own religion is from the outset raised to the status of a super-system. What seems to be tolerance proves in practice to be a sort of conquest by embrace, an integration through relativisation and loss of identity.

2. THE CRITICAL ECUMENICAL POSITION

a. i. In place of an indifferentism for which everything is equally valid we need to posit something more in the nature of *indifference* towards alleged orthodoxy that sets itself up as the measure of the salvation or damnation of human beings and that sets out to enforce its claim to truth with power and means of compulsion.

ii. In place of a relativism, for which there is no Absolute, we need to posit something more in the nature of a sense of combined *relativity*, on the one hand, in the face of all human pretensions to absoluteness, which prevents a productive co-existence of the various religious, and, on the other, *relationality*, which enables one to see every religion as a web of connections.

iii. In place of a syncretism, in which everything imaginable and unimaginable is mixed together and fused, we need rather to posit something in the nature of a synthesis of all confessional and religious antagonisms, that still every day cost blood and tears, so that peace reigns between the religions instead of war, hate and strife.

b. i. We cannot have too much patience and religious freedom in the face of all religiously motivated impatience. No betrayal of *freedom* for the sake of freedom!

ii. The opposite is, however, also true: no betrayal of truth for the sake of freedom! The question of truth cannot be trivialised or sacrificed in the interests of some Utopia of future world unity and a religion of world unity, In the Third World, where people still remember the history of colonialism and the history of the missions bound up with it, such a Utopia is rightly seen as a threat to the culturo-religious identity of the rising nations.

iii. As Christians we are challenged, in the spirit of a *freedom* founded on

Christ, to think afresh about the question of *truth*. For, unlike caprice, freedom is not simply freedom *from* all ties and duties, in any negative sense, but it is at the same time a freedom *for* a new responsibility: towards our fellow human beings, ourselves, the Absolute. True freedom is, therefore, freedom for truth.

c. i. The Christian possesses no monopoly of truth, and certainly has no right to invoke some pluralism of taste in order to renounce the *confession of truth*; dialogue and witness are not mutually exclusive. The witness to truth includes the courage to recognise and to articulate untruth.

ii. The boundaries between truth and untruth pass *through one's own present* religion. It follows that criticism of other positions is justifiable only on the basis of decisive self-criticism. This too is the only way in which integration of the values of other religions can be advocated. This means that not everything is equally true and good even in religions, there is false and bad in teaching about faith and morals, in religious rites and customs, institutions and authorities. Naturally this applies to Christianity too.

d. The need to discern between true (good) and false (bad) religion in all religions is what makes an inter-religious criteriology an urgent task, the content of which can only be indicated:

e. i. In virtue of the general principle of ethics a religion is true and good when and to the extent that it is *humane* and that it protects and promotes rather than suppresses and destroys humanity.

ii. In virtue of the general criterion of religion, a religion is good and true when and to the extent that it remains true to its own *origin* or *canon*—its authentic being, the normative Scripture or pattern on which it bases its appeal.

iii. In virtue of the specific criterion of Christianity, a religion is true and good when and to the extent that it allows traces of Christ to be detected in its teaching and practice. This criterion can be applied *directly* only to Christianity—the self-critical question can be put whether and how far Christianity is in any way Christian. The same criterion can indeed also be applied to the other religions, but *indirectly*—and without arrogance: by way of clarifying the question whether and to what extent we can detect something of the spirit in other religions (especially in Judaism and Islam) that we characterise as Christian.

3. a. What is proclaimed today as 'brand-new' teaching often proves to be the old teaching from the liberal Protestant stable. Such people do indeed hear God speaking through Jesus 'as well' but have abandoned his normativity and 'finality' (conclusiveness). They have put him on the level of other prophets alongside others (Christ together with other religions or other

revealers, saviours, Christs) and so have lost all criteria for the discernment of spirits. Against such liberalism the protest of Karl Barth and 'dialectical theology' (Rudolf Bultmann and Paul Tillich) was a necessary corrective. To go back in this direction is no progress.

b. Any theologian who is not prepared to give up this normativity and finality of Christ does so not because it is only through Christ as a critical catalyst that the other religions can 'adapt themselves to our modern technology', but because otherwise he or she would be abandoning the central declaration of the Scriptures that go to make up the New Testament. For the whole of the New Teastament—like it or not—Jesus is normative and definitive: he alone is the Christ of God (the oldest as well as the briefest confession of faith in the New Testament is just this: Jesoūs Kyrios), he is the 'way, the truth and the life'.

c. Holding fast to this two thousand years old conviction of truth—without anguish or apologetic concern, but on good ground, in the way that Jews, Muslims, Hindus and Buddhists do to theirs—is, however, in no way identical with some theological 'imperialism' and 'neo-colonialism', which denies other religions their truth and rejects other prophets and seers. If one is to avoid the basic flaws in either the absolutist-exclusivist or the relativistic-inclusivist positions, one must distinguish the view from without and the view from within (or however else one cares to put it). This is the only way in which one can come to a nuanced answer to the question of the truth of religions.

d. Looked at from outside, observed as it were from the viewpoint of comparative religion, it goes without saying that there are *different true religions*: religions that, with all their ambivalence, correspond to at least certainly basically defined general (ethical and religious) criteria. There are different ways of salvation (with different ways of representing salvation) to the one goal, and these in part overlap and can in any case enrich each other. Yet the dialogue between these religions by no means demands the giving up of the standpoint of faith. For:

e. Looked at from inside, from the viewpoint of the believing Christian orientating him- or herself by the New Testament, therefore myself as an affected and challenged human being, there is a *true religion*: Christianity, in so far as it witnesses to one true God as he has declared himself in Jesus Christ. The one true religion in no ways excluded truth in the other religions but can let others be: as religions *true up to a point* ('conditionally'—or some such— true). So far as they do not directly contradict the Christian message, these religions can complete, correct and deepen the Christian religion.

4. WHERE DOES A DIALOGUE WITHOUT A CONVICTION OF FAITH LEAD?

a. Anybody who renounces the normativity of his or her own tradition and takes as his or her point of departure the equal validity of the different 'Christs' (Jesus, Moses, Muhammad, Gautama):

i. clearly presupposes as a result something that would not be unconditionally desirable even as the end-product of a long process of understanding—such a method seems to be *a prioristic*:

ii. requires of the other non-Christian parties what most of them reject, namely, that they should from the outset give up their belief in the normativity of their own message and their own bringers of salvation and take up the (typically Western and modern) standpoint of the basic equality of the various ways: such a way seems to be *unrealistic*;

iii. requires Christians themselves to demote Jesus Christ to the status of a provisional messiah and to give up the conviction of faith offered and demanded from the New Testament onwards (because springing from the normative and definitive Word of God given with Jesus) in favour of a levelling down of Jesus Christ to the other bearers of revelation and bringers of salvation ('Kyrios Jesoūs', on the same level as 'Kyrios Kaísar' or 'Kyrious Gautama'): such a stance would have to be characterised as *non-Christian* (and, it goes without saying, without any question of a heresy hunt);

iv. juxtaposes the various guiding figures as if they did not stand in a historical dependence on each other (whether Moses and Jesus, or Jesus and Muhammad) and were not honoured in completely different ways within their own religions (as different as the positions of Moses in Judaism, of Jesus in Christianity, or Muhammad in Islam or of Gautama in Buddhism): such a way of looking at things seems to be *unhistorical.*

b. The upshot of all this for practice is that anybody, whether as a Christian or not, who makes such a standpoint his or her own runs the risk of (willingly or unwillingly) distancing him—or herself from his or her own community of faith, indeed essentially of giving up his or her own religion. But the dialogue between the religions is not advanced by a few Western (or Eastern) intellectuals agreeing together. There is scarcely a need to engage in discussion if there is in the end nothing normative and definitive in any religion. Yet the Christian community of belief may allow itself to be persuaded to replace an ecclesio-centrism with a Christo-centrism or theo-centrism (which for Christians amount to the same thing!) but they are hardly likely to be persuaded to take up some vague soterio-centrism. Practice should not be made the norm of theory undialectically and social questions be exponded as the basis and centre of the theology of religions.

5. WHERE DOES A DIALOGUE ON THE BASIS OF A CONVICTION OF FAITH LEAD?

a. Anybody who stands by the normativity of his or her own tradition and yet is open to other traditions:

i. starts off from the given and commits any final result and any agreement about the relationship of Jesus Christ and Muhammad (to take the Christian-Muslim dialogue as an example) wholly to the process of the dialogue and the understanding that emerges: a decidedly *a posteriori* approach;

ii. from the outset allows the partner in dialogue his or her stance of faith and first expects of him or her only unconditional readiness to hear and to learn, unrestricted openness that includes a transformation of both partners in the course of the process of mutual understanding; a *patiently realistic* way;

iii. acknowledges from the outset his or her own conviction of faith that for him or her Jesus is the Christ and so is normative and definitive, but he or she also takes very seriously the function of a Muhammad as an authentic (post-Christian) prophet and his 'warning' about a declension from belief in one God in Christianity: a self-critically *Christian* standpoint;

iv. sees the various traditions, their origins and their bearers of salvation in their context and according to the standing they enjoy (Muhammad does not stand in the same place in Islam as Christ does in Christianity, for he did not wish himself to be a Christ but the Qur'an), so that a nuanced view of the way in which the different traditions are inter-woven becomes possible: a strongly *historical* way of looking at things even though it *is* anchored in the faith of all concerned;

b. the significance of this for *practice* is this: anybody who makes such a basic attitude his or her own, whether as a Christian or not, can combine commitment to faith and readiness to understand, religious loyalty and intellectual honesty. He or she has a critically reflective tie to his or her community and is trying simultaneously in regard to his or her as well as to the other community of faith not only to interpret something afresh but to change it—with a developing ecumenical community in view. It is in a similar spirit that for now going on for half a hundred years a few convinced Catholics and Protestants, rooted in their respective traditions and yet self-critical, have begun to speak with each other, and, precisely to the extent that they have remained true to their own communities of faith, have changed themselves and their partners—and, in due course, both church communities. What we can hope, therefore, is that some equivalent process will develop between the world religions, even if over a longer time-scale.

By way of Conclusion

Have I not delineated the differences between the two methods rather too sharply? A great deal of what goes on in the actual practice of dialogue is much simpler, and many Christians will no doubt be able to agree on the following:

– We no longer want to tread our own Christian way stubbornly dogmatic and blind to other ways, without understanding, tolerance or love for them.

– On the other hand, we do not want to become so disappointed with our own way and be fascinated by the novelty of another that we change to that other way.

– We do not want just to put what we have learned from the other ways alongside our previous faith in some externally additive manner.

– No, rather than this what we want is, out of our very Christian commitment, to allow ourselves to be continuously changed and transformed as we press on our own way in constant readiness to learn, so that the old faith is not destroyed but enriched. This is the 'way of creative transformation' (Cobb), the way of adventurous Christian faith that continually opens up in ecumenical commitment.

Is this an entirely new task? By no means.

Is this not exactly what our forbears in the Church of antiquity did, the apologists and the Alexandrians Clement and Origen, when they encountered the neo-Platonic Stoic ways and worked out an ecumenically theological paradigm suitable to their age?

Did not Augustine and Thomas, confronted with a new Romano-German world, have to think theology through afresh in a process of transformation that was the way to a paradigm suitable for the Latin West?

Did not Luther and the Reformers have to allow themselves to be changed when in the great crisis of medieval theology and Church it became necessary to look back to the original gospel?

The Christian churches have lost a great deal of credibility in the course of encountering the world religions for the first time in the age of our modern paradigm, of belief in science and technology, colonialism and imperialism. This is the time—the time of our post-modern, post-colonial, polycentric age—to begin the dialogue with world religions afresh.

Translated by John Maxwell

Contributors

MICHAEL von BRÜCK was born in 1949. He is a Lutheran pastor from East Germany who has for the past five years lectured at the Gurukul Lutheran Theological College and Research Institute in Madras, India, as well as being a research scholar at the University of Madras. He has pursued studies in Indian philosophy (especially Advaita Vedānta and Mahayana Buddhism) and yoga. He has also spent a lot of time studying (Zen) in Japan. Besides his academic activities he has followed courses in meditation and yoga and inter-religious study weeks in Tibetan monasteries, Hindu ashrams and such like. In 1985 he began being visiting professor in a seminar on religious studies at the university of Hamburg. His publications include: *Möglichkeiten und Grenzen einer Theologie der Religionen* (1970) and articles on comparative trinitarian and advaita theologies, comparisons between Hindu and Christian religions, and aspects of Indian philosophy in various Western and Eastern journals.

JULIA CHING was born in Shanghai, China. She studied in Asia, the United States, and Europe, and received her doctorate from the Australian National University in Canberra, where she was also a lecturer in Asian Civilisations. She later taught at Columbia University and at Yale University. She is also an associate member of the Institute of Oriental Religions of Sophia University in Tokyo and is at present professor of religious studies at the University of Toronto. She has published in many professional journals, and her most recent books are *To Acquire Wisdom: the Way of Wang Yang-ming* (1976), a study of the fifteenth-century Chinese philosopher and *Confucianism and Christianity a Comparative Study* (1977).

CALID DURÁN was born in Morocco. Between 1957 and 1960 he studied Islamic science and Oriental languages in Pakistan, then political science and sociology in Bonn and Berlin. He was visiting professor at the Islamic Research Institute and lecturer in the department of sociology at the university of Islamabad between 1968 and 1975. Since 1978 he has been scientific collaborator at the German Oriental Institute in Hamburg. His publications include *Muhammad Iqbal and Ahmad Amin—A Comparative Study* (1976); *Die Politische Rolle des Islam* (1978); *Afghanistan's Struggle for National Liberation* (1980); *Islam and Civilization* (1982); *Re-Islamisierung und Entwicklungspolitik* (1982); *Das ist mein Islam* (1982); as well as various articles on aspects of Islamic history and thought in Tunisian, Swiss and Spanish journals.

PAULOS MAR GREGORIOS B.A. (Goshen); M.Div (Princeton); S.T.M. (Yale); Th.D. (Serampore); Th.D. (honoris causa, Budapest); Th.D. (h.c. Leningrad); Th.d. (h.c. Prague), was born in August, 1922. He is Metropolitan of Delhi and the North, Orthodox Syrian Church of the East, President of the World Council of Churches, Geneva, Principal of the Orthodox Theological Seminary, Kottayam, Vice-Chairman of the Kerala Philosophers' Congress. Recent publications include *Science for Sane Societies* (1980); *Cosmic Man* (1980); *The Indian Orthodox Church, An Overview* (1982).

WANG HSIEN-CHIH lives and works in Taiwan, Republic of China. He gained his B.S. in physics at the National Taiwan University in 1964, his M.Div. at Tainan Theological College and Seminary in 1968, his S.T.M. at the General Theological Seminary, New York, in 1973, and his D.Th. at South East Asian Graduate School of Theology in 1978. Between 1973 and 1985 he was successively lecturer, associate professor and professor of theology at Tainan Theological College, Taiwan. His publications include *The Concept of Nature in Tao-Teh-Chin and its Theological Meanings* (1978); *The Issues of Nature, God and Ideal of Society in the Ancient Chinese Culture* (1982); *The Role of Confucianism* (1983); *Martin Luther and Dietrich Bonhoeffer: A Taiwanese Perspective* (1984); *A Critical Reflection on the Methods of Phenomenology, Hermeneutics and the Idea of Contextualization in Religious and Theological Studies* (1984); *Some Perspectives on Theological Education in the Light of Homeland Theology in the Taiwanese Context* (1984).

ANTHONY JOHNS was born in London, U.K., in 1928. He studied at the

School of Oriental and African Studies, University of London, and gained a
B.A. in Malay and Arabic. He wrote his Ph.D. on 'Sufism in the Malay
World'. He is at present Fellow of the Institute for Advanced Studies, The
Hebrew University of Jerusalem, (1985) and head of the Southeast Asia
Centre, Faculty of Asian Studies, Australian National University. His
academic interests include Qur'anic exegesis and Islamic spirituality, Islam in
Southeast Asia, and contributions to a Christian understanding of Islam.
Recent publications include *Islam in Asia* (volume II) edited with R. Israeli
(1984); 'Joseph in the Qur'an: Dramatic Dialogue, Human Emotion and
Prophetic Wisdom' *Islamochristiana* 6 (Rome 1981). He is due to publish
'Variations on theme: Fakhr al-Din al-Razi's treatment of the Qur'anic
presentations of the episode of Abraham and his guests' in *Mideo* (Mélange
Dominicain d'Etudes Orientales) (medio 1985), Cairo.

PAUL F. KNITTER served as a Divine Word Missionary before assuming a
position at Xavier University, Cincinnati, Ohio in 1975, where he is presently
professor of Theology. He studied at the Gregorian University in Rome and
the University of Marburg, West Germany (Th.D.) He has published
Towards a Protestant Theology of Religions (1974), *No Other Name? A
Critical Survey of Christian Attitudes Toward the World Religions* (1985,
and various articles dealing with religious pluralism and interreligious
dialogue.

HANS KÜNG was born in Sursee, Switzerland, in 1928. He has been
professor of fundamental theology in the Catholic faculty of the university of
Tübingen since 1960; professor of dogmatic and ecumenical theology and
director of the institute for ecumenical research since 1963; extra-faculty
professor of ecumenical theology and director of the institute for ecumenical
research in the university of Tübingen since 1980. His most important
publications include: *Justification* (1964); *Council and Reunion* (1961);
Structures of the Church (1965); *The Church* (1967); *Infallible?* (1971); *On
Being a Christian* (1977); *Does God Exist?* (1980); *Eternal Life* (1984).

SHU-HSIEN LIU was born in Shanghai, China, in 1934, is married with two
sons, and is professor and chairman of the philosophy department in the
Chinese University of Hong-Kong. His publications include (in Chinese) *New
Philosophical Methods and Convictions in a Changing World* (1966); *An
Introduction to the Philosophy of Culture* (1970); *The Contemporary
Significance of Traditional Chinese Philosophical Wisdom* (1974); *Chinese
Philosophy and China's Modernization* (1980); *The Development and
Completion of Chu Hsi's Philosophical Thought* (1982).

BITHIKA MUKERJI was educated at Allahabad University. Her first thesis was written under the guidance of Prof. A. C. Mukerji, a leading neo-Vedantist of his time. She was invited to lead a Seminar and participate in a Graduate Programme in Bossey, Geneva during the year 1972-73. She was at McMaster University from 1973-77 writing her second thesis on the Ontology of Bliss. She was invited to attend the Zweites christlichfernöstliches Religionsgespräch der Stiftung Oratio Dominica in November 1984. The topic of her paper was 'Advaitic Experience and Cosmic Responsibility'. Dr. Mukerji was teaching in the Department of Philosophy in the Benares Hindu University from where she retired in December 1984. Her publications include *Neo Vedanta & Modernity* (1983); *Introduction to the Heritage of the Hindus* (to be published in 1986).

SEYYED HOSSEIN NASR was born in 1933. He studied physics and mathematics at M.I.T. where he graduated in 1954; did advanced studies at Harvard University where he received his M.A. and his Ph.D. in the history of science and philosophy with special emphasis upon Islamic science in 1958. He is at present University Professor of Islamic Studies, George Washington University. He has delivered, among others, the following famous lectures: the Iqbal Lecture, Pakistan, 1966; the Charles Strong Memorial Lectures, Australia, 1970; the Azad Memorial Lecture, India, 1975; the Gifford Lectures, University of Edinburgh, 1981 (he was the first Muslim ever to give this most famous and prestigious of all lectures on religion in the West). His publications include *Ideals and Realities of Islam* (also in Arabic, French, Spanish, Italian and German); *Introduction to Islamic Cosmological Doctrines* (also in Persian); *Man and Nature: The Spiritual Crisis of Modern Man* (also in French, Italian, Portugese and Spanish); *Knowledge and the Sacred; Islamic Art and Spirituality.*

SERI PHONGPHIT was born in 1947 in Sakonnakhon, Thailand. He gained his licentiate in Philosophy and Theology in Rome 1972, and his D.Phil. in the Hochschule fuer Philosophie Munich in 1978. He is Associate Professor in Philosophy, Thammasat University, Bangkok. He assists educational programmes and the Appropriate Theology programme of the Catholic Council of Thailand for Development. He is a board member of: The Thai Interreligious Commission for Development; the Coordinating Group for Religion and Society, and the Justice and Peace of Thailand. He has published books and articles in the Thai language, as well as his dissertation *'The Problem of Religious Language: A Study of Buddhadasa Bhikkhu and Ian Ramsey as Models for Mutual Understanding of Buddhism and Christianity'* (1978).

ALOYSIUS PIERIS, S.J., a Sri Lankan Jesuit, is the founder-director of the Tulana Research Centre in Kelaniya near Colombo. A Classical Indologist specialised in Buddhist Philosophy, he is now engaged in a vast research programme on medieval Pali (Buddhist) philosophical literature on which he has begun publishing a series of papers. He edits *Dialogue,* an international review for Buddhists and Christians published by the Ecumenical Institute, Colombo. He has written extensively on Missiology, Theology of Religions, Asian Theology of Liberation and on Buddhology. He is the visiting Professor of Asian Religions and Philosophies at the East Asian Pastoral Institute, Manila. A Theological consultant of the Christian Workers Fellowship (CWF) since 1968, he is engaged in Buddhist-Marxist-Christian dialogue.

LEROY ROUNER is Professor of Philosophical Theology at Boston University, Director of the Institute for Philosophy and Religion, and general editor of Boston University Studies in Philosophy and Religion. He graduated from Harvard College (A.B., 1953), Union Theological Seminary (B.D., *summa cum laude,* 1958), and Columbia University (Ph.D., 1961). He was Assistant Professor of Philosophy and Theology at the United Theological College, Bangalore, India, from 1961 to 1966. He is editor of the Hocking Festschrift, *Philosophy, Religion, and the Coming World Civilization* (1969), and (with John Howie) of *The Wisdom of William Ernest Hocking* (1978), as well as author of *Within Human Experience: The Philosophy of William Ernest Hocking* (1969) and *Return Home in Peace: The Christian Contribution to a World Community* (forthcoming). He was Visiting Professor of Philosophy at the University of Hawaii in 1982.

SULAK SIVARAKSA is coordinator of the Asian Cultural Forum on Development (ACFOD), Bangkok, visiting Professor to a few Thai, American and European Universities where he mainly teaches Buddhism and Philosophy. In 1983 he was one of the four Buddhists invited to attend the World Assembly of The World Council of Churches at Vancouver. His latest publications in English are *Siamese Resurgence; A Buddhist Vision for Renewing Society; Religion and Development.*

NEW TITLES FROM SCM PRESS

MARCH

Connections: The Integration of Theology and Faith
J L Houlden   paper   £5.95

Soul making: the Desert Way of Spirituality
Alan Jones   paper   £6.95

From Early Judaism to Early Church
D S Russell   paper   £4.50

Old Testament Law
Dale Patrick   paper   £8.50

APRIL

Government by the People?
Paul Rowntree Clifford   paper   £6.95

Theology on the Way to Emmaus
Nicholas Lash   paper   £10.50

Wilfred Cantwell Smith: A Theology for the World
Edward J Hughes   paper   £8.95

The Prayers of the Bible
R E Clements   paper   £7.95

New volumes for important series

Theological Dictionary of the Old Testament Volume 5
G J Botterweck and H Ringgren   cased   £25.00

Hermeneia: Ignatius of Antioch
William R Schoedal   cased   £32.00

Hermeneia: II Corinthians 8 & 9
Hans Dieter Betz   cased   £25.50

SCM PRESS LTD
26-30 TOTTENHAM ROAD LONDON N1 4BZ

CONCILIUM

CONCILIUM

CONCILIUM 1985

*All back issues are still in print: available from bookshops (price £3.95)
or direct from the publisher (£4.45/US$7.70/Can$8.70 including postage
and packing).*

**T. & T. CLARK LTD, 59 GEORGE STREET,
EDINBURGH EH2 2LQ, SCOTLAND**